Eldon Edmundson, Jr., PhD
Dennis McCarty, PhD
Editors

D0127952

Implementing Evidence-Based Practices for Treatment of Alcohol and Drug Disorders

Implementing Evidence-Based Practices for Treatment of Alcohol and Drug Disorders has been co-published simultaneously as *Journal of Addictive Diseases*, Volume 24, Supplement Number 1 2005.

Pre-publication REVIEWS, COMMENTARIES, EVALUATIONS . . .

"This book PROVIDES REAL-WORLD, PRACTICAL INFORMATION for improving substance abuse treatment and for increasing the adoption of evidence-based practices among clinicians. It identifies and illustrates potential pitfalls in these processes, but also suggests opportunities for improvement and recommends methods for enhancing the successful adoption of new practices."

Carla A. Green, PhD, MPH
Senior Investigator
Center for Health Research
Kaiser Permanente Northwest

More pre-publication
REVIEWS, COMMENTARIES, EVALUATIONS . . .

"This book summarizes a federally supported collaborative initiative to try out technology transfer strategies designed to improve treatment practices and accountability in community settings. A RARE TREAT, the text introduces us to the collaborators, reports the results of an assessment of their efforts, and also familiarizes us with their activities by including the results of the evaluation research studies that they implemented."

Paula K. Horvatich, PhD
Director
Mid-Atlantic Addiction Technology
Transfer Center
Department of Addiction Psychiatry
Virginia Commonwealth University

The Haworth Medical Press®
An Imprint of The Haworth Press, Inc.

Implementing Evidence-Based Practices for Treatment of Alcohol and Drug Disorders

Implementing Evidence-Based Practices for Treatment of Alcohol and Drug Disorders has been co-published simultaneously as *Journal of Addictive Diseases*, Volume 24, Supplement Number 1 2005.

Monographic Separates from the *Journal of Addictive Diseases*

For additional information on these and other Haworth Press titles, including descriptions, tables of contents, reviews, and prices, use the QuickSearch catalog at http://www.HaworthPress.com.

The *Journal of Addictive Diseases* is the successor title to *Advances in Alcohol & Substance Abuse.**

Implementing Evidence-Based Practices for Treatment of Alcohol and Drug Disorders, edited by Eldon Edmundson, Jr., PhD, and Dennis McCarty, PhD (Vol. 24 Suppl. 1, 2005). *Strategies for improving the quality of substance abuse treatment by increasing the exchange between community-based service providers and the research community.*

Eating Disorders, Overeating, and Pathological Attachment to Food: Independent or Addictive Disorders?, edited by Mark S. Gold, MD (Vol. 23, No. 3, 2004). *Examines the relationship between overeating and substance abuse to support the hypothesis that some eating disorders are similar to addiction disorders.*

Addiction Treatment Matching: Research Foundations of the American Society of Addiction Medicine (ASAM) Criteria, edited by David R. Gastfriend, MD (Vol. 22 Suppl. 1, 2003). *Focuses on the ins and outs of the ASAM Criteria–the state-of-the-art in addictions placement matching.*

Effects of Substance Abuse Treatment on AIDS Risk Behaviors, edited by Edward Gottheil, MD, PhD (Vol. 17, No. 4, 1998). *In this important book, you will discover drug abuse treatment methods that will reduce the number of injection episodes and reduce injection use in higher risk settings, such as shooting galleries, thereby reducing your clients risk of infection.*

Smoking and Illicit Drug Use, edited by Mark S. Gold, MD (Vol. 17, No. 1, 1998). *"Based on an understanding of the brain biology of reward, Gold and his colleagues provide policymakers, clinicians, and the public with the best-ever look at the reason why 90% of the nation's more than 60 million cigarette smokers want to quit but have trouble achieving that life-saving goal." (Robert L. DuPont, MD, President, Institute for Behavior and Health, and Professor of Psychiatry, Georgetown University School of Medicine, Rockville, MD). Focuses on the addictive properties of the numerous constituents of tobacco smoke and nicotine dependency.*

The Integration of Pharmacological and Nonpharmacological Treatments in Drug/Alcohol Addictions, edited by Norman S. Miller, MD, and Barry Stimmel, MD (Vol. 16, No. 4, 1997). *Summarizes and provides the groundwork for future considerations in developing and integrating medications with the standard of care for addictions treatment.*

Intensive Outpatient Treatment for the Addictions, edited by Edward Gottheil, MD, PhD (Vol. 16, No. 2, 1997). *"An invaluable source of up-to-date information on important issues relating to IOP, including the active ingredients of successful IOP, the effectiveness of IOP, causes of early dropout, and the impact of psychiatric status and motivation for change on outcomes for patients." (Stephen Magura, PhD, Director, Institute for Treatment Research, National Development & Research institutes, Inc., New York)*

The Neurobiology of Cocaine Addiction: From Bench to Bedside, edited by Herman Joseph, PhD, and Barry Stimmel, MD (Vol. 15, No. 4, 1997). *"Provides an excellent overview of advances in the treatment of cocaine addiction." (The Annals of Pharmacotherapy)*

The Effectiveness of Social Interventions for Homeless Substance Abusers, edited by Gerald J. Stahler, PhD, and Barry Stimmel, MD (Vol. 14, No. 4, 1996). *"Any policymaker or administrator seeking to have a positive impact on the complex problems of this population would be well-advised to thoroughly digest the contents of this volume." (Journal of Behavioral Health Services & Research (formerly the Journal of Mental Health Administration))*

Experimental Therapeutics in Addiction Medicine, edited by Stephen Magura, PhD, and Andrew Rosenblum, PhD (Vol. 13, No. 3/4, 1995). *"Recommended for any clinician involved in caring for patients with substance abuse problems and for those interested in furthering research in this discipline." (The Annals of Pharmacotherapy)*

Comorbidity of Addictive and Psychiatric Disorders, edited by Norman S. Miller, MD (Vol. 12, No. 3, 1993). *"A wealth of factual information . . . it should be included in the library of every psychiatric hospital because it is an excellent reference book." (Israel Journal of Psychiatry)*

Cocaine: Physiological and Physiopathological Effects, edited by Alfonso Paredes, MD, and David A. Gorlick, MD, PhD (Vol. 11, No. 4, 1993). *"The broad range of psychiatric and medical consequences of the epidemic of cocaine use described in this volume should jolt everyone toward increasing strategies to educate, motivate, and stimulate health practitioners at all levels." (Perspectives on Addictions Nursing)*

What Works in Drug Abuse Epidemiology, edited by Blanche Frank, PhD, and Ronald Simeone, PhD (Vol. 11, No. 1, 1992). *"An excellent reference text not only for researchers and scholars, but also for administrators, policymakers, law enforcements agents, and health educators who value the importance of research in decisionmaking at both the micro and macro levels of the ever-growing substance abuse speciality." (International Journal of Epidemiology)*

Cocaine, AIDS, and Intravenous Drug Use, edited by Samuel R. Friedman, PhD, and Douglas S. Lipton, PhD (Vol. 10, No. 4, 1991). *"Examines what has been successful in treatment and prevention and raises issues to promote greater research in the fields for improved treatment and prevention of drug abuse and HIV-infection." (Sci-Tech Book News)*

Behavioral and Biochemical Issues in Substance Abuse, edited by Frank R. George, PhD, and Doris Clouet, PhD* (Vol. 10, No. 1/2, 1991). *"An excellent overview of the power of genetic experimental designs, the results that can be generated as well as the cautions that must be observed in this approach." (Contemporary Psychology)*

Addiction Potential of Abused Drugs and Drug Classes, edited by Carlton K. Erikson, PhD, Martin A. Javors, PhD, and William W. Morgan, PhD* (Vol. 9, No. 1/2, 1990). *"A good reference book for anyone who works in the drug abuse field, particularly those who have responsibilities in the area of community education." (Journal of Psychoactive Drugs)*

Alcohol Research from Bench to Bedside, edited by Enoch Gordis, MD, Boris Tabakoff, PhD, and Markku Linnoila, MD, PhD* (Vol. 7, No. 3/4, 1989). *Scientists and clinicians examine the exciting endeavors in science that have produced medical knowledge applicable to a wide spectrum of treatment and prevention efforts.*

AIDS and Substance Abuse, edited by Larry Siegel, MD* (Vol. 7, No. 2, 1988). *"Contributes in a worthwhile fashion to a number of debates." (British Journal of Addiction)*

Pharmacological Issues in Alcohol and Substance Abuse, edited by Barry Stimmel, MD* (Vol. 7, No. 1, 1988). *"Good reference book for the knowledge of the pharmacology of certain drugs used in treating chemically dependent cases." (Anthony B. Radcliffe, MD, Physician in Charge, Chemical Recovery Program, Kaiser, Pontana, California)*

Children of Alcoholics, edited by Margaret Bean-Bayog, MD, and Barry Stimmel, MD* (Vol. 6, No. 4, 1988). *"This comprehensive volume examines significant research and clinical development in this area." (T.H.E. Journal)*

Cocaine: Pharmacology, Addiction, and Therapy, edited by Mark S. Gold, MD, Marc Galanter, MD, and Barry Stimmel, MD* (Vol. 6, No. 2, 1987). *"Diagnosis and treatment methods are also explored in this highly useful and informative book." (Journal of the American Association of Psychiatric Administrators)*

Alcohol and Substance Abuse in Women and Children , edited by Barry Stimmel, MD* (Vol. 5, No. 3, 1986). *Here is a timely volume that examines the problems of substance abuse in women and children, with a particular emphasis on the role played by the family in the development and perpetuation of the problem.*

Controversies in Alcoholism and Substance Abuse, edited by Barry Stimmel, MD* (Vol. 5, No. 1/2, 1986). *"Thorough, well-informed, and up-to-date." (The British Journal of Psychiatry)*

Alcohol and Substance Abuse in Adolescence, edited by Judith S. Brook, EdD, Dan Lettieri, PhD, David W. Brook, MD, and Barry Stimmel, MD* (Vol. 4, No. 3/4, 1985). *"Contains considerable information that would be useful to mental health clinicians and primary care physicians who deal extensively with adolescents." (The New England Journal of Medicine)*

Alcohol and Drug Abuse in the Affluent, edited by Barry Stimmel, MD* (Vol. 4, No. 2, 1984). *"A valuable contribution to drug abuse literature presenting data on a hitherto under-researched population of drug users." (British Journal of Addiction)*

Cultural and Sociological Aspects of Alcoholism and Substance Abuse, edited by Barry Stimmel, MD* (Vol. 4, No. 1, 1984). *Experts explore the relationship of such factors as ethnicity, family, religion, and gender to chemical abuse and address important implications for treatment.*

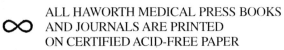

Implementing Evidence-Based Practices for Treatment of Alcohol and Drug Disorders

Eldon Edmundson, Jr., PhD
Dennis McCarty, PhD
Editors

Implementing Evidence-Based Practices for Treatment of Alcohol and Drug Disorders has been co-published simultaneously as *Journal of Addictive Diseases*, Volume 24, Supplement Number 1 2005.

The Haworth Medical Press®
An Imprint of The Haworth Press, Inc.

New York • London • Victoria (AU)
www.HaworthPress.com

Published by

The Haworth Medical Press®, 10 Alice Street, Binghamton, NY 13904-1580 USA

The Haworth Medical Press® is an imprint of The Haworth Press, Inc., 10 Alice Street, Binghamton, NY 13904-1580 USA.

Implementing Evidence-Based Practices for Treatment of Alcohol and Drug Disorders has been co-published simultaneously as *Journal of Addictive Diseases*, Volume 24, Supplement Number 1 2005.

The development, preparation, and publication of this work has been undertaken with great care. However, the publisher, employees, editors, and agents of The Haworth Press and all imprints of The Haworth Press, Inc., including The Haworth Medical Press® and Pharmaceutical Products Press®, are not responsible for any errors contained herein or for consequences that may ensue from use of materials or information contained in this work. Opinions expressed by the author(s) are not necessarily those of The Haworth Press, Inc. With regard to case studies, identities and circumstances of individuals discussed herein have been changed to protect confidentiality. Any resemblance to actual persons, living or dead, is entirely coincidental.

Cover design by Jennifer M. Gaska.

Library of Congress Cataloging-in-Publication Data

Implementing evidence-based practices for treatment of alcohol and drug disorders / Eldon Edmundson, Jr., Dennis McCarty, editors.
     p. cm.
     "Co-published simultaneously as Journal of Addictive Diseases, Volume 24, Supplement Number 1 2005."
     Includes bibliographical references and index.
     ISBN-13: 978-0-7890-3151-8 (hard cover : alk. paper)
     ISBN-10: 0-7890-3151-5 (hard cover : alk. paper)
     ISBN-13: 978-0-7890-3152-5 (soft cover : alk. paper)
     ISBN-10: 0-7890-3152-3 (soft cover : alk. paper)
     1. Drug abuse–Treatment. 2. Alcoholism–Treatment. 3. Substance abuse–Treatment. 4. Evidence-based medicine. I. Edmundson, Eldon. II. McCarty, Dennis, Ph. D. III. Journal of addictive diseases.
     [DNLM: 1. Substance-Related Disorders–therapy. 2. Alcoholism–therapy. 3. Evidence-Based Medicine. WM 270 I335 2005]
RC564.I48 2004
362.29–dc22
                                         2005019204

Indexing, Abstracting & Website/Internet Coverage

This section provides you with a list of major indexing & abstracting services and other tools for bibliographic access. That is to say, each service began covering this periodical during the year noted in the right column. Most Websites which are listed below have indicated that they will either post, disseminate, compile, archive, cite or alert their own Website users with research-based content from this work. (This list is as current as the copyright date of this publication.)

(continued)

(continued)

(continued)

Special Bibliographic Notes related to special journal issues (separates) and indexing/abstracting:

- indexing/abstracting services in this list will also cover material in any "separate" that is co-published simultaneously with Haworth's special thematic journal issue or DocuSerial. Indexing/abstracting usually covers material at the article/chapter level.
- monographic co-editions are intended for either non-subscribers or libraries which intend to purchase a second copy for their circulating collections.
- monographic co-editions are reported to all jobbers/wholesalers/approval plans. The source journal is listed as the "series" to assist the prevention of duplicate purchasing in the same manner utilized for books-in-series.
- to facilitate user/access services all indexing/abstracting services are encouraged to utilize the co-indexing entry note indicated at the bottom of the first page of each article/chapter/contribution.
- this is intended to assist a library user of any reference tool (whether print, electronic, online, or CD-ROM) to locate the monographic version if the library has purchased this version but not a subscription to the source journal.
- individual articles/chapters in any Haworth publication are also available through the Haworth Document Delivery Service (HDDS).

Implementing Evidence-Based Practices for Treatment of Alcohol and Drug Disorders

CONTENTS

ABOUT THE EDITORS

Eldon Edmundson, Jr., PhD, is an Associate Professor in the Department of Public Health and Preventive Medicine at Oregon Health and Science University in Portland, Oregon. He directed the Oregon Practice Improvement Collaborative, which conducted studies at the local, regional, and state level, to identify key ingredients leading to the successful adoption of science-based practices by community-based treatment agencies. Dr. Edmundson has experience in building research and practice consortiums, developing and implementing effective health professional training programs, establishing research platforms that focus on improved delivery of services, and assisting agencies to implement evidence-based practices. From 1985 to 1996, he served as Dean and Professor for the College of Health Science at Boise State University in Idaho.

Dennis McCarty, PhD, is a Professor in the Department of Public Health and Preventive Medicine at Oregon Health and Science University in Portland, Oregon, and Principal Investigator for the Oregon Node of the National Drug Abuse Treatment Clinical Trails Network. From 1989 to 1995, he directed the Massachusetts Bureau of Substance Abuse Services for the Massachusetts Department of Public Health. Dr. McCarty collaborates with policymakers in state and federal government and with community-based programs to study the organization, financing, delivery, and effectiveness of publicly funded substance abuse treatment services. He has served on two Institute of Medicine committees.

Preface

An Institute of Medicine report, *Bridging the Gap Between Practice and Research*, observed a disconnect between the development of research-based treatment innovations and the application of those techniques to treatment for alcohol and drug disorders.[1] Practitioners and programs were challenged to use research and to improve the quality of care they provide. Federal agencies for research (National Institute on Drug Abuse and National Institute on Alcohol Abuse and Alcoholism) and service (Center for Substance Abuse Treatment) were encouraged to facilitate the application of research findings in clinical settings. The report catalyzed federal investment in strategies to facilitate adoption and diffusion of science-based interventions.

The Center for Substance Abuse Treatment developed Practice Improvement Collaboratives and asked them to identify technology transfer strategies that supported use of desirable practices and improved accountability. Practitioners partnered with investigators in regional and state initiatives to assess needs, explore strategies to foster counselor training and support the use of therapeutic techniques emerging from research settings in community-based treatment programs. At the same time, the Veterans Health Administration (VA) invested in the Quality Enhancement Research Initiative (QUERI) and developed modules to promote substance abuse intervention in primary care, foster the use of science-based practices for treatment of alcohol and drug disor-

---

Awards from the Center for Substance Abuse Treatment (UD1 T1 12904; PIC-STAR-SC-03-044) and the Robert Wood Johnson Foundation (46876, 50155) supported the development of this document.

[Haworth co-indexing entry note]: "Preface." Edmundson, Jr., Eldon, and Dennis McCarty. Co-published simultaneously in *Journal of Addictive Diseases* (The Haworth Medical Press, an imprint of The Haworth Press, Inc.) Vol. 24, Supplement No. 1, 2005, pp. xix-xxii; and: *Implementing Evidence-Based Practices for Treatment of Alcohol and Drug Disorders* (ed: Eldon Edmundson, Jr., and Dennis McCarty) The Haworth Medical Press, an imprint of The Haworth Press, Inc., 2005, pp. xv-xviii. Single or multiple copies of this article are available for a fee from The Haworth Document Delivery Service [1-800-HAWORTH, 9:00 a.m. - 5:00 p.m. (EST). E-mail address: docdelivery@haworthpress.com].

xv

ders, and to improve care for alcohol and drug dependent patients with comorbid conditions.[2]

Implementing and sustaining evidence-based practices depend on practitioner and treatment program factors including a stable workforce with the knowledge, skills and attitudes to meet the needs of the clients; capability to respond to sporadic changes in funding for treatment; capacity to respond to the changing client population needs in the types of and location of the service needed; and capability to monitor program delivery and measure client progress in treatment.

This Supplement to the *Journal of Addictive Diseases* provides managers, clinicians and other key stakeholders with results from knowledge adoption studies that focused on the specifics of diffusion of innovation into substance abuse treatment agencies. Papers examine practice improvement collaboratives, test training and mentoring strategies to support adoption, and assess the roles that clinical orientation and philosophy have on clinician readiness to change and to use evidence-based practices. Methadone maintenance is an example of an evidence-based practice that is not widely available and the barriers to the expansion of methadone services are explored within the VA system of care.

Cotter, Bowler, Mulkern, and McCarty describe the development and early implementation of Practice Improvement Collaboratives. They found environmental adoption, formal organizational structures and processes, stability in the workforce, and targeted and consistent collaborative goals as important processes for early adoption. They discuss the usefulness of the investigator-provider-policy maker model in furthering integration and sustaining of evidence-based substance abuse treatment practices and the value of system support for science-based practices.

Ager and colleagues provide insights on the effectiveness of an intensive 2-day training and a booster session for improving the knowledge, attitudes and behaviors of clinicians using Motivational Enhancement Therapy. They discuss opportunities and challenges that brief MET training activities face in enhancing clinician knowledge, skills, and attitudes about MET. This work provides information to agencies on possible strategies for adopting and sustaining MET use.

Eliason, Arndt, and Schut examine the role that agency beliefs about the similarities of treatment philosophies therapists say they use and the actual techniques or tools reported using in daily practice. Critical to the adoption process, they discuss the variability of the therapies agencies provide to clients and the belief by some that they do in fact use evidence-based practices, yet, what may happen is that agencies use a "modified" version of an evidence-based practice to better fit the agencies needs.

Another strategy for supporting adoption of evidence-based practices is the use of Opinion Leaders to complement intensive training. Peters and his associates discuss the use of manuals, opinion leaders, and training as strategies to support adoption. Adoption of an evidence-based manualized treatment for individuals with co-occurring mental health and drug use disorders was greatest in treatment programs where peer opinion leaders were trained first. Conceptually, this article points out the use of "change leaders" as important to the adoption process.

Characteristics of the workforce, particular clinicians and their readiness for change, can also facilitate or inhibit adoption. Toriello and colleagues found interesting differences in the readiness to change–women and counselors who were not African-American were more willing to change clinical practices. Clinical orientation (traditional or non-traditional) was not influential. This information provides important insights on the development of targeted strategies that utilizes the differences in clinician demographics and training.

The final paper draws on work within the VA to improve the quality of services for veterans dependent on opioids. Trafton, Humphreys, Kivlahan, and Willenbring surveyed the directors of addiction treatment programs about the use of evidence-based practice guidelines. Programs that included methadone maintenance were larger and the directors were more likely to have an academic affiliation, research experience, and confidence in clinical research. Moreover, they also were more accurate in their assessments of the level of empirical support for specific clinical practices. The investigators suggest that experience with clinical research facilitates the adoption of evidence-based practices.

This compilation of papers provides practitioners, policy makers, and treatment programs insights into challenges and opportunities promoting the diffusion of evidence-based practices for treatment of alcohol and drug disorders. It develops insights for the provider, investigator, and policy maker to consider when developing national, state, regional and agency strategies to enhance treatment effectiveness. Strategies to promote organizational change are emerging as keys.

The Practice Improvement Collaboratives served as an incubator nourishing early exploration of methods to promote the use of science-based practices. Three recent models outline relationships between organizational and clinician factors and the adoption of evidence-based practices.[3-6] The models provide guidance to investigators and treatment programs about issues to consider as programs respond to "external and internal pressures" to alter and improve the delivery of care.

Addiction treatment services continue to mature and evolve. The Center for Substance Abuse Treatment partnered with the Robert Wood Johnson Foundation in the development of the Network for the Improvement of Addiction Treatment (NIATx). The Network continues the alliance between research and practice and focuses on improving access to care and retention in treatment. Five key principles support agency change and promotes increased access and retention: understanding and involving the customer, fixing key problems, use of powerful change leaders, getting ideas from outside the organization or field, and being able to conduct test and practice change rapidly. These models and concepts provide a strategic and tactical framework that the field can use to support the adoption of evidence-based practices and other innovations.

Eldon Edmundson, Jr., PhD
Dennis McCarty, PhD

REFERENCES

1. Institute of Medicine. Bridging the Gap Between Practice and Research: Forging Partnerships with Community-Based Drug and Alcohol Treatment. Washington, DC: National Academy Press, 1998.

2. Finney JW, Willenbring ML, Moos RH, Feussner JR, Demakis JG, Kizer KW. Improving the Quality of VA Care for Patients With Substance-Use Disorders: The Quality Enhancement Research Initiative (QUERI) Substance Abuse Module. Medical Care. 2000; 38(6) (Supplement I)):I-105-I-113.

3. Gustafson DH, Sainfort F, Eichler M, Adams L, Bisognano M, Steudel H. Developing and Testing a Model to Predict Outcomes of Organizational Change. Health Services Research. 2003; 38(2):751-76.

4. Simpson DD. A Conceptual Framework for Transferring Research to Practice. Journal of Substance Abuse Treatment. 2002; 22:171-82.

5. Thomas CP, Wallack S, Lee SS, McCarty D, Swift R. Research to Practice: Factors Affecting the Adoption of Naltrexone in Alcoholism Treatment. Journal of Substance Abuse Treatment. 2003; 24(1):1-11.

6. Thomas CP, McCarty D. Adoption of drug abuse treatment technology in specialty and primary care settings. Harwood HJ. Immunotherapies and Depot Medications for the Treatment and Prevention of Drug Dependence. Washington, DC. National Academy Press. 2004.

Practice Improvement Collaboratives: An Overview

Frances Cotter, MA, MPH
Suzanne Bowler, PhD
Virginia Mulkern, PhD
Dennis McCarty, PhD

SUMMARY. The Center for Substance Abuse Treatment created Practice Improvement Collaboratives (PICs) to promote implementation of evidence-based practices for the treatment of alcohol and drug dependence through partnerships of practitioners, investigators, policy makers

Frances Cotter is affiliated with the Center for Substance Abuse Treatment, Rockville, MD 20857.

Suzanne Bowler is affiliated with Northrop Grumman Health Solutions, Rockville, MD 20850.

Virginia Mulkern is affiliated with the Health Services Research Institute, Cambridge, MA 02140.

Dennis McCarty is affiliated with Oregon Health & Science University, Portland, OR 97239.

Address correspondence to: Dennis McCarty, Department of Public Health & Preventive Medicine, CB669, Oregon Health & Science University, 3181 SW Sam Jackson Park Road, Portland, OR 97239 (E-mail: mccartyd@ohsu.edu).

The PIC Developmental Workgroup stimulated preparation of case studies and identified developmental variables. The authors gratefully acknowledge their enthusiastic support.

Preparation of the manuscript was supported through cooperative agreements and contracts with the Center for Substance Abuse Treatment.

[Haworth co-indexing entry note]: "Practice Improvement Collaboratives: An Overview." Cotter, Frances et al. Co-published simultaneously in *Journal of Addictive Diseases* (The Haworth Medical Press, an imprint of The Haworth Press, Inc.) Vol. 24, Supplement No. 1, 2005, pp. 1-14; and: *Implementing Evidence-Based Practices for Treatment of Alcohol and Drug Disorders* (ed: Eldon Edmundson, Jr., and Dennis McCarty) The Haworth Medical Press, an imprint of The Haworth Press, Inc., 2005, pp. 1-14. Single or multiple copies of this article are available for a fee from The Haworth Document Delivery Service [1-800-HAWORTH, 9:00 a.m. - 5:00 p.m. (EST). E-mail address: docdelivery@haworthpress.com].

and consumers. Early implementation experiences within 11 PICs are examined and factors that facilitated and inhibited program maturation are identified. Case studies, structured interviews and a review of presentations and reports were used to document developmental processes. Successful development consistently required environmental adaptation, construction of formal organizational structures and processes, recruitment and retention of membership, and implementation of activities that fostered the mission of the Collaboratives. The Collaboratives provide a useful model for promoting the application of research-based innovations to practice and policy in the treatment of alcohol and drug abuse and dependence. *[Article copies available for a fee from The Haworth Document Delivery Service: 1-800-HAWORTH. E-mail address: <docdelivery@ haworthpress.com> Website: <http://www.HaworthPress.com> © 2005 by The Haworth Press, Inc. All rights reserved.]*

KEYWORDS. Practice Improvement Collaboratives, evidence-based practices, application of research to practice

The distance between practitioners and regular use of evidence-based therapies may be especially noticeable among programs treating substance abuse. Although slow adoption of research-based medicine contributes to poor quality care, increased morbidity and mortality and unnecessary costs throughout the health care system in the United States,[1] traditional alcohol and drug abuse interventions persist long after research identifies more effective therapies.[2] Practitioners do not perceive the research as relevant, have little access to the research literature and have not participated in the design and completion of the investigations. The Institute of Medicine, therefore, recommended that the Substance Abuse and Mental Health Services Administration and the National Institutes on Health facilitate linkages between research and practice to promote adoption of research findings for the treatment of alcohol and drug abuse and to encourage practice relevant research.[2]

The Center for Substance Abuse Treatment responded. Its National Treatment Plan recommended collaboration among service providers, academic institutions, researchers and other stakeholders and encouraged incentives for treatment programs to apply evidence-based practice innovations.[3] The Practice Improvement Collaboratives program (originally named Practice Research Collaboratives) catalyzed partnerships among practitioners, researchers, policy makers, and consumers and promoted adoption of research-based practice innovations. This paper provides an overview of the Practice Improvement Collaboratives program (PICs or Collaboratives). Goals for the Collaboratives are outlined. Interviews and case studies identified factors that facilitated and inhibited development of the PICs. Implementation lessons are abstracted and next steps are outlined.

COLLABORATIONS BETWEEN SCIENCE AND PRACTICE

The Practice Improvement Collaborative project grew from roots with origins in the literature on diffusion of technology, community prevention and treatment initiatives, and federally sponsored treatment demonstrations. Assessments of the adoption and diffusion of technology for the treatment and prevention of alcohol and drug abuse[4-7] provided an empirical basis for the PIC emphasis on adoption of innovation. Studies of practice innovation suggested that implementation and institutionalization are more likely when adoption strategies are multifaceted, stakeholder needs are addressed and multiple system components support change.[8-12] Monographs,[13] journal issues[14,15] and journal papers[11] described community prevention and treatment initiatives and helped the PIC anticipate the complexities encountered in the development and evaluation of community collaborations. Finally, PIC construction drew on experiences with community treatment demonstrations that tested services for pregnant and parenting women,[16] evaluated programming for homeless individuals.[17,18] and promoted central intakes and shared information systems.[19] These demonstrations illustrated the challenges encountered in application of treatment innovations to substance abuse treatment for hard to serve groups of patients. The evaluation of the homeless demonstrations[20] and work on the implementation of evidence-based practices in mental health treatment[12,21] highlighted the need to maintain fidelity to the intervention within complex systems of care. Addiction Technology Transfer Centers drew on this literature and articulated seven principles of effective technology transfer within organizations that treat alcohol and drug dependence.[22]

Practitioner/researcher collaborations can facilitate the adoption of research findings in clinical settings and foster more practice relevant research. Substance abuse treatment practitioners are more likely to adopt new practices when they collaborate in the development and testing of these practices.[23] Collaborations between clinical and research staff are most effective when the environment is supportive, formal infrastructures are developed to support the partnership, the mission is clearly articulated, and cohesiveness is promoted.[8,9,24] Provider efforts to implement research-based practice innovations also promote attention to the fidelity and sustainability of the interventions, test implementation strategies, and articulate new research questions.[10-12,20,21,25] Effective alliances may increase resources for treatment programs and enhance therapist skills,[2] promote practitioner involvement in the construction of research questions,[10,25] and foster practitioner understanding of application of research methods.[10,26]

PRACTICE IMPROVEMENT COLLABORATIVES

The Practice Improvement Collaboratives program emphasized practitioner and researcher alliances to implement evidence-based practices and promote a balanced partnership of research teams and community treatment programs. Each Collaborative addressed five requirements: (1) build sustainable formal organizations, (2) operate in partnership with providers, researchers, policymakers, and consumers, (3) respond to the needs and interests of community stakeholders, (4) promote the adoption of evidence-based practices that address community needs and priorities, and (5) evaluate implementation and provide feedback to the membership on the development and maturation of the Collaboration.[27]

Applicants received awards in 1999, 2000, and 2001 and built organizational infrastructures, expanded networks and identified best practice priorities. Table 1 lists the sites and summarizes sponsorship, service area and their evidence-based practices. CSAT also supported a national resource center.

The grantees were usually academic organizations (n = 7) but included a substance abuse provider association, a treatment provider, a city health department, and a state office of substance abuse services in partnership with the state provider association. Six projects operated statewide and seven focused on regional areas or special populations.

PIC governing bodies used different organizational structures, but each included an advisory board, a decision making group, committees or project teams, and an administrative structure. Advisory bodies (e.g., Advisory Board/Council, Planning Committee, Partnership Council) met two or three times a year and provided guidance and input on major decisions. Decision-making groups (e.g., Executive Committee, Steering Committee, Board of Directors, or Core Network Group) convened monthly to review and approve ongoing plans and meetings, forums, and the development of communication systems. Committees and Project

TABLE 1. Characteristics of the Practice Improvement Collaboratives

State	Grantee	Service Area	Evidence-Based Practices
AZ	U. of Arizona	Statewide	1. Integrated treatment for co-occurring disorders 2. Motivational interviewing 3. Family-focused services assessment
CA	UCLA Integrated Substance Abuse Programs	Los Angeles	1. Africentric Motivational Intervention 2. Use of ASI 3. Treatment of stimulant disorders 4. Treatment for people with disabilities
CA	San Francisco Dept of Public Health	San Francisco	1. Pharmacotherapy 2. Standardized automated assessments 3. Relapse prevention
FL	U. of South FL	Tampa Bay area	1. Integrated treatment for co-occurring disorders in criminal justice system 2. Gender-sensitive treatment for women in criminal justice system
GA	Morehouse School of Medicine	West Central Georgia	1. Parenting skill development 2. Relapse prevention
IA	U. of Iowa	Statewide	1. Integrated treatment for co-occurring disorders 2. Gender-sensitive treatment for women with children
IL	Illinois Treatment Alternatives for Safe Communities	Chicago	1. Methadone maintenance 2. Women in recovery 3. Pharmacological treatment for criminal justice populations 4. Infectious disease treatment
LA	Council on Alcohol and Drug Abuse	New Orleans area	1. Motivational enhancement therapy for adolescents 2. Motivational enhancement therapy for previously incarcerated individuals
NC	Governor's Institute on Alcohol and Substance Abuse	Statewide	1. Relapse prevention 2. Co-occurring disorders 3. Motivational interviewing
NY	NY State Office of Alcoholism and Substance Abuse Services and the Alcoholism and Substance Abuse Providers of NY	Statewide	1. Standardized traumatic brain injury screening 2. Mental health screening 3. ASAM level of care criteria
OR	Oregon Health & Science University	Statewide	1. Motivational interviewing 2. Automated assessment tools
OR/WA	Oregon Health & Science University	Urban American Indians in Portland, Salem and Seattle	1. Motivational Enhancement Therapy for American Indian youth 2. Use of ASI in adolescent treatment 3. Cognitive behavioral therapy for American Indian youth
PA	Institute for Research, Education and Training in the Addictions	Statewide	1. Relapse prevention for offenders 2. Performance monitoring systems

Teams met as needed and were tasked with specific activities (network development, knowledge adoption) or addressed special populations (e.g., women and children, persons with co-occurring substance abuse and mental disorders, and persons in the criminal justice system). Finally, an administrative team (e.g., Operations Committee, Project Management Team, or Coordinating Center) handled day-to-day operations. Collaboratives guided operations with principles, operating procedures, rules, or by-laws. Membership was diverse and included treatment providers (including health plans and provider associations), investigators, state and county policymakers, and consumers.

The evidence-based practices selected for training and implementation varied. Arizona, Los Angeles, New Orleans, North Carolina, Oregon and Urban Indian Collaboratives directed attention toward the use of motivational interviewing or motivational enhancement therapy. Integrated services for individuals with mental health and substance abuse disorders were emphasized in Arizona, Tampa Bay, Iowa, and North Carolina; New York State stressed improvements in mental health screening in substance abuse treatment. Standardized assessment and placement criteria received attention in the Los Angeles, San Francisco, New York State, Oregon, and Urban Indian Collaboratives. Arizona, Chicago, Tampa Bay, Georgia, and Iowa addressed services for women and families. Relapse prevention was a focus in Pennsylvania, North Carolina, San Francisco, and Georgia. New York and Los Angeles tried to improve services for individuals with disabilities. Finally, pharmacological services received attention in San Francisco and Chicago.

To document PIC development, the project sites and the Center for Substance Abuse Treatment (CSAT) established the Developmental Project Workgroup. Each PIC participated and the workgroup stimulated preparation of case studies, constructed a framework for reporting case studies, prepared a descriptive overview and articulated lessons learned during early development. Developmental processes were abstracted from structured interviews with investigators and project directors and from site descriptions and quarterly reports. Because community implementation and evaluation activities are complex and progress may be incremental, it is critical to preserve early development activities in the public record; too often, these lessons are not shared.[26]

PIC DEVELOPMENT AND IMPLEMENTATION LESSONS

Administrative structures evolved and strategies were modified as Collaboratives matured from proposals into fully functioning organizations. Successful development consistently required environmental adaptation, infrastructure construction, membership recruitment and retention, and mission relevant practice improvement activities.[8,9,24]

Environmental Adaptation. The PICs made strategic use of environmental assets and resolved liabilities. Assets included shared values and interests, proximity to resources, history of collaboration, and recognized leadership. Community leaders who shared interest in results-oriented research and commitment to the adoption of evidence-based practices provided environmental support. Los Angeles, Chicago, Florida, New York, North Carolina, Oregon, Pennsylvania, Urban Indian, and San Francisco forged strong ties with state and local substance abuse, mental health, and criminal justice agencies. The New York, North Carolina, Oregon, and Urban Indian Collaboratives built on existing ties with the Governor's Council on Alcohol and Drug Abuse Programs and the state provider associations. Collaboratives shared and learned from each other in cross-site meetings. Linkages with the Addiction Technology Transfer Centers (Iowa, New York, Oregon, and Pennsylvania) and the National Drug Abuse Clinical Trials Network (Los Angeles, Florida, New York, and Oregon) were useful. A PIC director observed that linkages with other projects ". . . enabled us to capitalize on existing energy, institutions, and processes."

Environmental challenges included disinterested stakeholders, limited resources, geography, and time constraints. Lack of endorsements and disinterest from local political leaders and established research groups inhibited start-up. To overcome these hurdles, the emerging coalitions (a) increased their public visibility through conferences and media coverage (b) nurtured relationships with potential stakeholders (individuals and organizations) through courtesy visits, networking, and providing individualized assistance on immediate needs, and (c) personally invited participation on governing bodies and advisory groups. The Arizona Collaborative, for example, involved key policymakers in a conference of practitioners and researchers to encourage interaction and networking. Sites linked with other community resources and identified additional funding to confront limited financial resources. Long distances and geographic barriers interfered with development in rural areas (Arizona, Georgia, Iowa, North Carolina, and Oregon). Solutions included scheduling meetings in the middle of the state to reduce travel time, holding general meetings and committee meetings the same day, and communicating through conference calls, video network trainings, and E-mail. Time was the most precious and limited resource. Directors of provider organizations and treatment facilities often had difficulty finding time for Collaborative activities. Compensation for administrative activities and meeting time facilitated participation among executive directors. Another strategy was to invite clinical supervisors to participate because they had fewer external commitments.

A focus on building the collaborative enterprise served the Practice Improvement Collaboratives well. They generated considerable local interest in evidence-based practices and brought together individuals and organizations that historically had few working relationships. At the system level, the collaborations were associated with substantive initiatives, including:

- State adoption of Evidence-Based Practice as a guiding principle for design and funding of treatment services (AZ).
- Collaboration with the Single State Agency Director to develop a statewide science-to-service network (IA).
- Sponsorship of statewide Best-Practices Committee on Methadone (IL).
- Establishment of the Addiction Leadership Group (composed of payers, providers, researchers, and policy makers) to develop a performance monitoring system for statewide application (PA).
- Leadership in the formation of a statewide Practice Improvement Unit, encompassing all of the substance abuse agency's science-to-service initiatives (NY).
- Adaptation of motivational effectiveness therapy for use with American Indians (Urban American Indian Collaborative).

Organizational Structures. Three common themes characterized organizational development: administration, flexibility, and collaborative structures. Sites found they needed strong administrative teams to coordinate activities, communicate with members about these activities and other relevant information, and insure follow-through. Collaboratives evolved from small simple organizations to complex structures that accommodated increased membership and responded to priorities. West Central Georgia, for example, began operations as a management team and grew into a formal structure with a Board of Directors, committees to address specific issues, and a grants management team. Other Collaboratives (e.g., Tampa Bay, Iowa, and San Francisco) added committees, teams, and interest groups to respond to stakeholders needs and interests. New York State Collaborative built a two-tiered organization–a statewide Consortium balanced with seven regional Practice Research Networks. The lead agency (the state's alcohol and drug treatment authority) and its partner (the state provider association) formed project management teams to coordinate activities in each of the seven regions.

Organizational procedures that modeled the collaboration process were implemented. Representatives from the research, policy, and provider communities provided balanced leadership and co-chaired committees and boards. Members participated in the construction of the organizational structure, articulation of mission and goals, and selection of knowledge application and dissemination activities and events. Development of the organizational structures reflected the leadership qualities found in other successful enterprises (experts, protectors, facilitators and innovators).[28] Technology transfer works best when leaders allow the process to be participatory rather than "top down." [5,29]

Membership Recruitment and Retention. Collaborations are effective when participants join and become invested in the mission and activities. Strategies for membership recruitment and retention were both open and selective. Membership was open to providers, researchers, policymakers, and consumers committed to program goals and willing to contribute expertise, feedback, contacts, or resources. Collaboratives also took care to represent the geographic, racial/ethnic, and socioeconomic diversity of their target communities, especially underrepresented groups. Arizona's Implementation Team, for example, reflected the state's geographic and racial/ethnic diversity, in particular Hispanic/ Latinos and American Indians. The Urban Indian Collaborative sought providers experienced with Indians and recruited stakeholders who were Indians or were knowledgeable about the needs of urban and rural Indians.

Recruitment required multiple outreach strategies. Sites conducted informal surveys to identify candidates. Media, posters displays at meetings, and informational mail-outs publicized the Collaboratives. Conferences and events attracted participants. Collaboratives visited local treatment organizations and conducted focus groups with policymakers, researchers, providers, and consumers to encourage input and participation. Tampa Bay used surveys to identify and recruit local substance abuse service and advocacy organizations and criminal justice agencies. The New Orleans Collaborative used media announcements and mail-outs to promote participation; letters invited potential candidates to join the 15-member Steering Committee. Consumer recruitment was also challenging. Collaboratives sought individuals sufficiently strong in their recovery to participate without suffering a relapse yet close enough to treatment experiences to understand patient needs. Tampa Bay recruited six consumers, gave them active roles as consumer representatives in the Core Network Group and other committees, and paid them for their participation.

Collaboratives offered valued benefits to sustain member investment including assistance with proposal development, on-site and video network seminars and trainings, free or low-cost continuing education units. The Urban Indian Collaborative used video trainings on primary care and addiction treatment, treatment for depressed alcoholics, effective interventions for American Indian youth, and provided on-site and/or electronic case consultations. Iowa and San Francisco sponsored skills building workshops on women, substance abuse, and corrections.

Long-term relationships were central to developing mutual trust. One director noted that building relationships with individuals in the community was time-consuming but well worth the effort because of the gain in goodwill. Through working for years in their communities, directors gained reputations for credibility, dedication, and trustworthiness and thus the support of members. Their reputations are one of the elements crucial for successful technology transfer.[30]

Collaborative Activities. Formal needs assessments often facilitated implementation of evidence-based practices. The assessments identified community priorities for improving clinical practices and service delivery. Stakeholders participated in the design and completion of the needs assessments through focus groups, interviews, and provider surveys. Several sites (i.e., Iowa, Oregon, Pennsylvania, and the Urban Indian Collaborative) combined their data with existing statewide needs assessments. Frequently identified priorities included services for persons with co-occurring substance abuse and mental disorders, services for women and children, and culturally sensitive treatment.

The needs assessments guided selection of evidence-based practices for implementation and plans for practice improvement projects. Governing bodies formally endorsed practice improvement agendas that formed the basis of the "practice improvement" plan–short- and long-term strategies to implement and evaluate coordinated knowledge dissemination, exchange and adoption activities. Newsletters, web sites, and state of the art conferences increased practitioner awareness of the evidence-based practices. Networking and mentoring fostered special interest groups and facilitated close working relationships. Training and technical assistance promoted evidence-based practices (e.g., screening and assessment for individuals with co-occurring mental health and substance abuse, motivational interviewing) and evaluations monitored implementation and adoption.

In brief, Collaboratives nourished organizational cultures emphasizing cohesion rather than competition, participation rather than exclusion, and egalitarianism rather than hierarchy. Directors cultivated these norms and values through communication, consensus decision-making, fostering autonomy, and assisting stakeholders. The activities created common experiences and fostered mutual support and dependence.

Implementation of Evidence-Based Practices. In addition to their networking and dissemination activities, limited studies tested strategies to implement evidence-based practices in community treatment organizations. Implementation strategies included training opinion leaders, training-the-trainers, workshops with and without booster sessions or other enhancements, use of video and Internet, academic detailing, researchers in residence, and organizational change. A variety of evidence-based practices were promoted (e.g., motivational interviewing, gender-specific treatments, integrated care for co-occurring mental health and substance abuse problems, relapse prevention, cognitive behavioral therapy, and community reinforcement approaches). Finally, the Collaboratives engaged a diversity of patient populations–American Indian youth, African Americans, offenders and inmates, rural communities, women, adolescents, and persons living with chronic diseases (i.e., HIV/AIDS).

Most of the implementation studies used a single intervention group and focused on changes in attitudes and behaviors occurring after the intervention/training. Approximately one-quarter of the studies (n = 9), however, used more rigorous designs that compared standard training with an enhanced intervention, including four which randomly assigned (individuals or groups) to the intervention. The evaluations suggest that characteristics of the community treatment organizations and their practices complicated the implementation process. These included the prior training and experience of staff, processes for assigning clients to providers, data collection limitations, limitations related to the frequency and/or duration of treatment that could be reimbursed, and limited supervisory capacity. In many cases these limitations and complications could have been anticipated if a more extensive environmental scan had been conducted prior to implementation.

Supervisors require special attention. Organizations differ markedly in terms of the amount and nature of supervision provided. Learning new treatment approaches is a complicated business and frequently requires nuanced changes in provider behavior. Efforts need to be made to insure that appropriate supervision is available within the treatment organization or that it is provided in an ongoing fashion by the trainers.

Finally, implementation frequently included changes in the evidence-based intervention to make it more compatible with the perceived needs of the implementing organization or the population served. These changes ranged from minor modifications in the language of training materials to more substantial changes in training approaches, the treatment "dosage," or the expectations about the prior training and experience of staff providing services. By and large, the interventions implemented were complex packages and we have little knowledge of the "active ingredients" of each intervention. "Tweaking" evidence-based interventions, without a clear understanding of how these modifications change the intervention raises important questions about fidelity and the degree to which these changes may have an impact on service effectiveness.

DISCUSSION

The Practice Improvement Collaborative program engaged constituents and built infrastructures to improve treatment through evidence-based practices. Collaboratives attended to the qualities that characterize successful collaboration–environmental adaptation, development of organizational structures, membership recruitment and retention, and activities consistent with the needs and mission of the alliance. Sites constructed formal organizations with missions, goals, and objectives, and included stakeholders from all sectors, including underserved populations. Organizational structures were flexible enough to incorporate new components and respond to specific participant interests. Project directors provided leadership through facilitation rather than control and were able to develop trust and nurturing relationships with individuals and organizations. Organizational cultures promoted and modeled collaboration. Membership benefits helped convince many that participation was to their advantage.

PICs learned that collaboration requires continued investments of time and resources. The rewards, however, were enthusiasm from practitioners, practice relevant research, and greater attention to the blending of practice and research. Practice Improvement Collaboratives offer a unique strategy for blending practice, research and policy. They show great potential for advancing the knowledge and understanding of how to and improve services through the transfer of evidence-based practices. Room's essay on the integration of practice and research, however, notes that the mix of practitioners, policy makers, consumers and investigators is inherently unstable and requires skill and energy to maintain.[26]

REFERENCES

1. Millenson ML. Demanding Medical Excellence. University of Chicago Press. Chicago. 1997.

2. Institute of Medicine. Bridging the Gap Between Practice and Research: Forging Partnerships with Community-Based Drug and Alcohol Treatment. Washington, DC. National Academy Press. 1998.

3. Substance Abuse and Mental Health Services Administration. Changing the Conversation–Improving Substance Abuse Treatment: The National Treatment Plan Initiative. Substance Abuse and Mental Health Services Administration. Rockville, MD. 2000; Report No: DHHS Publication No. SMA-00-3479.

4. Backer TE, Rogers EM, Sopory P. Designing Health Communication Campaigns: What Works? Thousand Oaks, Sage Publications. CA. 1992.

5. Backer TE, David SL. Synthesis of behavioral science learnings about technology transfer. In: Backer TE, David SL, Soucy G. Reviewing the Behavioral Science Knowledge Base on Technology Transfer. Rockville, MD. National Institute on Drug Abuse. 1995; pp. 262-279.

6. Brown BS. From research to practice: The bridge is out and the water's rising. Advances in Medical Sociology. 2000; 7:345-365.

7. Morgenstern J. Effective technology transfer in alcoholism treatment. Substance Use & Misuse. 2000; 35:1659-1678.

8. Butterfoss FD, Goohman RM, Wandersman A. Community coalitions for prevention and health promotion. Health Education Research. 1993; 8(3):315-330.

9. Butterfoss FD, Goodman RM. Community coalitions for prevention and health promotion: Factors predicting satisfaction, participation, and planning. Health Education Quarterly. 1996; 23(1):65-79.

10. Israel BA, Schulz AJ, Parker EA, Becker AB. Review of community-based research: Assessing partnership approaches to improve public health. Annual Review of Public Health. 1998; 19:173-202.

11. Jensen PS, Hoagwood KB, Trickett EJ. Ivory towers or earthen trenches? Community collaborations to foster real-world research. Applied Developmental Science. 1999; 3(4):206-212.

12. Torrey WC, Drake RE, Dixon L, Burns BJ, Flynn L, Rush AJ, Clark RE, Klatzker D. Implementing evidence-based practices for persons with severe mental illness. Psychiatric Services. 2001; 52(1):45-50.

13. Giesbrecht N, Rankin J. Reducing alcohol problems through community action research projects: Contexts, strategies, implications, and challenges. Substance Use & Misue. 2000; 35(1 & 2):31-53.

14. Allamani A, Casswell S, Graham K, Holder HD, Holmila M, Larsson S, Nygaard P. Introduction: Community action research and the prevention of alcohol problems at the local level. Substance Use & Misuse. 2000; 35(1 & 2):1-10.

15. Yin RK, Kaftarian SJ. Introduction: Challenges of community-based program outcome evaluations. Evaluation and Program Planning. 1997; 20(3):293-297.

16. Rahdert ER. Introduction to the perinatal-20 treatment research demonstration program. Treatment for drug-exposed women and their children: Advances in Research Methodology. Rockville, MD. National Institute on Drug Abuse. 1996. pp.1-5.

17. Argeriou M, McCarty D. The use of shelters as substance abuse stabilization sites. Journal of Mental Health Administration. 1993; 20:126-137.

18. Conrad KJ, Hultman CI, Lyons JS. Treatment of the Chemically Dependent Homeless: Theory and Implementation in Fourteen American Projects. Binghamton, NY: Haworh Press. 1993.

19. Guydish J, Muck R. Reorganizing publicly funded drug abuse treatment: The experience of ten target cities projects. Journal of Psychoactive Drugs. 1999; 31(3): 273-278.

20. Orwin RG. Assessing program fidelity in substance abuse health services research. Addiction. 2000; 95(Supplement 3):S309-S327.

21. Bond GR, Evans L, Salyers MP, Williams J, Kim HW. Measurement of fidelity in psychiatric rehabilitation. Mental Health Services Research. 2000; 2(2):75-85.

22. Addiction Technology Transfer Centers, The Change Book: A Blueprint for Technology Transfer. Kansas City, MO. Addiction Technology Transfer Center National Office. 2000.

23. Brown BS. Reducing impediments to technology transfer in drug abuse programming. Backer TE, David SL, Soucy G. Reviewing the Behavioral Science Knowledge Base on Technology Transfer. Rockville, MD. National Institute on Drug Abuse. 1995.

24. Mattessich P, Monsey BR. Collaboration: What Makes It Work–A Review of Research Literature on Factors Influencing Successful Collaboration. St. Paul, MN. Amherst H. Wilder Foundation. 1992.

25. Stoil MJ, Hill GA, Jansen, MA, Sambrano S, Winn FJ. Benefits of community-based demonstration efforts: Knowledge gained in substance abuse prevention. Journal of Community Psychology 2000;28(4):375-389.

26. Room R. Community action and alcohol problems: The demonstration project as an unstable mixture. Giesbrecht N, Conley P, Denniston RW, Gliksman L, Holder H, Pederson A, Room R, Shain M. Research, Action, and the Community: Experiences in the Prevention of Alcohol and Other Drug Problems. Rockville, MD: Office for Substance Abuse Prevention; 1990, pp.1-25.

27. Center for Substance Abuse Treatment. Bridging the Gap: Developing Community-Based Practice/Research Collaboratives. Rockville, MD: Center for Substance Abuse Treatment; 1999. Report No.: Guidance for Applications (GFA) No. TI 99-006.

28. Maccoby M. Why Work: Motivating and Leading the New Generation. New York: Simon & Schuster, Inc.; 1989.

29. Diamond MA. Organizational change as human process, not technique. Backer TE, David SL, Soucy G. Reviewing the Behavioral Science Knowledge Base on Technology Transfer. Rockville, MD: National Institute on Drug Abuse; 1995. pp.119-131.

30. Backer TE. Assessing and enhancing readiness for change: Implications for behavior change. Backer TE, David SL, Soucy G. Reviewing the Behavioral Science Knowledge Base on Technology Transfer. Rockville, MD: National Institute on Drug Abuse; 1995.

A Study on the Effectiveness of a Brief Motivational Enhancement Therapy Training

Richard Ager, PhD
Stephanie Roahen-Harrison, MPH
Paul J. Toriello, RhD
Patricia Morse, PhD
Edward Morse, PhD
Linton Carney, JD
Janet Rice, PhD
Patricia Kissinger, PhD

Richard Ager is affiliated with the Tulane University School of Social Work, 6823 St. Charles Avenue, New Orleans, LA 70118-5672.

Stephanie Roahen-Harrison, Janet Rice, and Patricia Kissinger are affiliated with the Tulane University School of Public Health and Tropical Medicine, Department of Epidemiology, 1140 Canal Street, Suite 2000, New Orleans, LA 70112.

Paul J. Toriello is affiliated with the Louisiana State University Health Sciences Center, Department of Rehabilitation Counseling, 1900 Gravier Street, New Orleans, LA 70112.

Patricia Morse is affiliated with the Louisiana State University Health Sciences Center, Department of Psychiatry, 1900 Gravier Street, New Orleans, LA 70112.

Edward Morse is affiliated with the Tulane University School of Medicine, Department of Pediatrics, 1430 Tulane Avenue, New Orleans, LA 70112.

Linton Carney is affiliated with AIDS Law of Louisiana, Inc., 144 Elk Place, Suite 1530, New Orleans, LA 70112.

Janet Rice is also affiliated with the Tulane University School of Public Health and Tropical Medicine, Departments of Biostatistics (Suite 2001) and Epidemiology (Suite 2000), 1140 Canal Street, Suite 2001, New Orleans, LA 70112.

Address correspondence to: Richard Ager at the above address (E-mail: ager@tulane.edu).

[Haworth co-indexing entry note]: "A Study on the Effectiveness of a Brief Motivational Enhancement Therapy Training." Ager, Richard et al. Co-published simultaneously in *Journal of Addictive Diseases* (The Haworth Medical Press, an imprint of The Haworth Press, Inc.) Vol. 24, Supplement No. 1, 2005, pp. 15-31; and: *Implementing Evidence-Based Practices for Treatment of Alcohol and Drug Disorders* (ed: Eldon Edmundson, Jr., and Dennis McCarty) The Haworth Medical Press, an imprint of The Haworth Press, Inc., 2005, pp. 15-31. Single or multiple copies of this article are available for a fee from The Haworth Document Delivery Service [1-800-HAWORTH, 9:00 a.m. - 5:00 p.m. (EST). E-mail address: docdelivery@haworthpress.com].

Available online at http://www.haworthpress.com/web/JAD
doi:10.1300/J069v24S01_02

SUMMARY. This study evaluated the effectiveness of a 2-day training and 4-hour booster, based on the Carkhoff Approach. It was designed to improve the knowledge, attitudes, and behaviors of Motivational Enhancement Therapy (MET) among a community-based sample of counselors serving adolescents and incarcerated or post-incarcerated substance abusers. Surveys were administered at 3 time points to an immediate training, delayed training and no training group. The 267 participants, representing over 40 agencies, were mostly female (68%) and African-American (60%). About half had a master's education (52%), and came from agencies with fewer than 25 employees (53%). Based on Generalized Estimating Equation analyses, training participants demonstrated improved MET knowledge, attitudes and behaviors, and maintained those changes for at least 4 months. The results suggest that a brief Carkhoff-based training protocol can facilitate the successful adoption of MET for a diverse sample of counselors of adolescent and post- or currently-incarcerated substance abusers. *[Article copies available for a fee from The Haworth Document Delivery Service: 1-800-HAWORTH. E-mail address: <docdelivery@haworthpress.com> Website: <http://www.HaworthPress. com> © 2005 by The Haworth Press, Inc. All rights reserved.]*

KEYWORDS. Drug abuse, psychotherapeutic techniques, professional development, clinical methods training, counselors

INTRODUCTION

Background and Purpose

Despite substantial gains made in developing evidence-based practices (EBP) for substance abuse treatment, there is limited adoption of these practices in community agencies.[1] Substance abuse counselors are increasingly pressured to demonstrate effectiveness. However, reviews of substance abuse treatment research indicate that many counselors continue to employ treatments with no empirical support.[2] Counselors may forgo use of EBPs due to poor compatibility with agency settings, the intervention may not be effective across diverse populations, or it may be too complex to implement.[1] Organizational barriers may interfere, or there may be philosophical differences between the EBP and the approach embraced by the agency or counselor. Certain facilitators of implementing effective practices may be absent from the work environment such as strong supportive opinion leaders, adequate training and supervision, or sufficient resources.[3]

Despite the importance of identifying methods to facilitate the adoption of proven treatments, there are few studies on the effectiveness of training strategies.[4,5] To address this problem, the Center for Substance Abuse Treatment funded 14 sites, called practice improvement collaboratives, to develop and evaluate methods for adopting EBPs. This study reports on a practice improvement collaborative in New Orleans which evaluated the effectiveness of a brief training protocol for an EBP called Motivational Enhancement Therapy (MET). The training was provided to substance abuse counselors serving adolescents and post- or currently incarcerated substance abusers. Through evaluating and identifying effective training approaches, these investigators hoped to improve methods used to adopt EBPs.

Adoption of EBPs

Motivational Enhancement Therapy (MET). MET is a brief psychotherapy that seeks to evoke motivation for change through clarifying client goals. Adapted from MI for use in the Matching Alcohol Treatments to Client Heterogeneity "MATCH" study,[6] MET will be treated as essentially the same approach as MI throughout this paper.[7] Derived from Rogerian and Social Psychology theory, MET experts contend that, with the counselor's direction, the client will innately attempt to resolve immobilizing ambivalence, and choose healthy aspirations over pathological behaviors. The counselor avoids pressing for healthy change because the client will argue the opposite side of that ambivalence–to not change. Rather, the counselor uses such techniques as reflective listening in a client-centered and directive manner to elicit the client's own reasons for change. Like other brief therapies, MET is a challenging approach to master, particularly for counselors accustomed to employing MET-inconsistent techniques such as confrontation, persuading, and asking closed-ended questions. There is good evidence from controlled studies that MET is effective in changing a broad range of problem behaviors with diverse populations.[8]

Training. The manner in which training is provided impacts the success of implementation. As described in the literature, substance abuse training is distinguishable primarily based on its dosage or intensity. Proponents of more intensive training generally argue that it should be agency-based, ongoing, involve considerable time,[9] and include all levels of the organization.[3] Less intensive training generally lasts 1-2 days, it is not ongoing, and the majority of the instruction is didactic. Proponents of intensive training argue that a brief 1- or 2-day workshop is insufficient to adequately train complex therapeutic behaviors such as MET, and it may even be damaging in that it can instill a false sense of competency.[10] Nevertheless, the vast majority of post-degree training occurs in these brief workshops and conferences, which necessitates the development of techniques to maximize their effectiveness.

Despite the strong support of many experts for extensive agency-based training programs, no empirical studies have evaluated their effectiveness. A number of studies have evaluated the effectiveness of workshops as a vehicle to teach therapeutic skills. In one investigation, child welfare workers reported improved attitudes and confidence about working with substance abusers following addictions-related training.[11] In another study, secretaries working in agencies that serve alcohol-abusing clients increased their knowledge and awareness of alcohol problems following a workshop in this area.[12] Crits-Christoph et al. evaluated therapist adherence and competence in 3 treatment modalities for cocaine abusers: supportive-expressive dynamic therapy, Cognitive Therapy, and 12-step drug counseling.[13] Global ratings of improvement for 65 counselors across four successive training cases indicated positive effects for only Cognitive Therapy.

Some studies specifically evaluated Motivational Interviewing (MI) training. Miller and Mount conducted a small study ($N = 15$) examining the effectiveness of a 2-day workshop.[10] Based on self-report questionnaires and coding of taped sessions before, just after and 4 months after training, attendees increased MI-consistent behaviors, although they retained pre-training levels of MI-inconsistent behaviors. Despite limited change, attendees reported that they had acquired competence in MI. A similar but larger study ($N = 44$) evaluated the impact of a 2-day workshop measuring pre- and post-training scores from a knowledge questionnaire and responses to clinical vignettes. The results indicated that counselors gained MI knowledge and skills as a result of training.[14] The changes reported in both studies appeared to be modest and further training seemed to be necessary before competency in MI could be achieved.

Two recent studies examined the impact of various training strategies, some of which included careful evaluation or supervision in addition to traditional didactic training. Sholomskas et al. evaluated 78 community-based substance abuse clinicians with regard to the impact of three different training conditions: Cognitive Behavioral (CB) manual, manual plus a CB training Web site, or manual plus a didactic seminar followed by supervised casework.[4] Based on independent ratings of structured role plays, the manual plus seminar and supervision showed greater improvement than the manual only condition. The Web condition scored in the middle. Miller, Yahne, Moyers, Martinez and Pirritano conducted a study with 140 licensed substance abuse professionals randomized to 5 training conditions: (a) clinical workshop; (b) workshop plus practice feedback; (c) workshop plus individual coaching; (d) workshop, feedback, and coaching; or (e) a waiting list self-guided training as the control.[15] Based on audio-taped practice samples at baseline, post-training, and 4, 8, and 12 month follow-up intervals, the 4 trained groups showed larger gains and the additional coaching and/or feedback amplified improvement. Together, these studies suggest that the more intensive the training, the better the improvement.

The training studies presented above sometimes mentioned a book, manual, or video tapes for the participants; but, little detail was provided on specifically of how the trainers were trained. This is particularly true with regard to the limited descriptions of the workshops, which were generally the heart of the training. Miller et al. were somewhat of an exception in that they provided some detail on supplemental training components (i.e., feedback and coaching).[15] However, very little information was provided with regard to the trainers' behaviors except mention that their workshop was structured so that 50% involved didactics and demonstration and 50% focused on direct practice skills. It is the intent of the current study to describe the major components of a training model, which includes a trainer's manual and checklist, to better clarify what is being evaluated. This approach asserts that unless the components of the workshop or supplemental trainings are carefully described, it is difficult to specifically identify what is effective.

Although intensive, ongoing, agency-based training may arguably yield better competencies, it is often not feasible due to cost and time restraints. Virtually all state psychotherapy licenses and certifications require continuing education hours to retain practitioner status. Brief trainings currently represent the primary method of continuing education programs. Consequently, research on enhancing the effectiveness of brief as opposed to intensive training may have broader applications in our current system of continuing education. The purpose of this study was to test whether a brief MET training could effectively instigate change in the counselor's knowledge, attitudes, and behaviors.

MATERIALS AND METHODS

Subjects

The 267 participants in this study were substance abuse counselors serving adolescents and/or currently- or post-incarcerated adults. A local community needs assessment of substance abuse professionals conducted in early 2000 indicated that their greatest training needs were in the treatment of these two target populations. Recruitment letters were sent to all substance abuse agencies, licensed social workers, and board certified substance abuse counselors primarily in the New Orleans metropolitan area. Follow-up phone calls and visits were made to agencies. With each contact, requests were made for referrals to further agencies or individuals who might be interested in participating.

Individuals were accepted into the study if they planned to live in southern Louisiana for at least the next year, at least 10% of their caseload was substance-involved adolescents (ages 13-18) and/or incarcerated/post-incarcerated individuals, and they used MET less than 90% of the time. Training was free, and participants with licenses or certifications in counseling, social work, nursing, or Louisiana substance abuse counseling received continuing education units for the hours they attended training. Participants provided written informed consent, and the research was approved by the Tulane University Human Subjects Institutional Review Board.

Measures

The instrument employed in this study took about 30-45 minutes to complete and included questions on demographics, work environment, barriers and facilitators to employing new treatment technologies, and MET knowledge, attitudes, and behaviors. The measures were first developed based on a literature search, and then revised following a careful review by a team of 10 researchers. The instrument was pretested by 10 counselors not participating in the study to improve its clarity.

Knowledge. Knowledge was measured with 11 questions on MET philosophy, principles, and techniques. The response format was either true-false or objective. A typical true-false question was "MET is a directive, yet client-centered counseling style." Scores were tallied by summing correct (score = 1) and incorrect (score = 0) items for a potential maximum score of 11. Based on Kuder Richardson reliability, the internal consistency of this instrument was $\alpha = .87$ ($n = 262$ baseline surveys) and the test-retest reliability for individuals not trained between Time 1 (T1) and Time 2 (T2), separated by 4 months, was $r = .61$ ($n = 132$).

Attitudes. The Attitude score was based on items assessing the respondents' eagerness to use MET or whether they saw MET as effective and sound. There were 6 attitude items, all employed a 5-point Likert scale ranging from "strongly disagree" to "strongly agree." One question was "I believe that MET is an effective treatment for substance-involved individuals." Scores were tallied by taking the mean of all item scores, for a range of 1 to 5. The internal consistency for this instrument was $\alpha = .82$ ($n = 265$) and the test-retest reliability for individuals not trained between T1 and T2 was $r = .69$ ($n = 132$).

Behaviors. There were 3 measures for MET behaviors. The first, Percent MET Used, was based on a question which inquired about the percent of time the counselor employed MET with ambivalent substance-involved clients. The response format was a 5-point Likert scale where 0 represented "never," 1 represented 1-25%, and 4 represented 76-100%. The test-retest reliability for individuals not trained between T1 and T2 was $r = .48$ ($n = 128$,). The second behavior measure, MET Techniques, was based on 8 MET practice behaviors. Using a 5-point Likert scale, response options ranged from "never use" (scored as "0") to "always use" (scored as "4"). Scores were tallied by taking the mean item score for all items. The internal consistency of this scale was $\alpha = .65$ and the test-retest reliability was $r = .54$ ($n = 132$).

The third MET behavior measure, Vignette Responses, was based on written responses to 3 open-ended clinical vignettes of fictional clients expressing ambivalence about their substance use. These responses were coded by 6 raters: 5 were MET trainers and the sixth was a licensed social worker and doctoral student trained in MET. Ratings were based on a 3-point scale, measuring whether the response was inconsistent with the MET approach (e.g., confrontational statements, closed-ended questions; rated as "1"), neither consistent with nor inconsistent with MET principles (e.g., a mixture of MET-consistent and MET-inconsistent statements; rated as "2"), or consistent with MET principles (e.g., open-ended questions, reflections, affirmations, summaries; rated as "3"). Scores were tallied by taking the mean of the item scores. Of the 1809 total scenarios (3 scenarios for 603 surveys collected over three time periods), 16.5% were missing or could not be coded. Raters were paired into dyads, and each dyad was responsible for independently rating one-third of the responses. Raters were blinded to time of the survey and intervention arm. The intraclass correlation coefficient (ICC) for the ratings was 0.68, based on a two-way random effects model, assuming a single rater and relative agreement, and pooled over time, scenario, and dyad. There was no substantial difference in the ICC by group, scenario, or time. After two more runs, the six raters achieved consensus by discussing any remaining discrepant ratings. Some knowledge items and vignettes were borrowed from the Arizona Practice Improvement Collaborative[16] and modified to fit the target population.

Procedures

Surveys. The surveys were mailed to 324 individuals, with several follow-up calls and visits to the agencies to facilitate completion. The return rate at T1 was 77%, T2 was 61%, and T3 was 51%. Given the analysis conducted for this study, generalized estimating equations, all but 6 participants were retained in the analysis. Comparison of those completing the T1 survey only, the T1 plus T2 surveys, and the T1 plus T2, plus T3 surveys found no differences on demographic or outcome variables. Subjects received $10 per survey completed, plus a $10 bonus if they completed all three.

Training. The training essentially followed the same procedures employed by the Motivational Interviewing Network of Trainers (MINT), which is similar to the Carkhuff Approach. While the MINT training protocol is not published, the Carkhuff Approach has extensive support for its effectiveness in training counselors, physicians, and numerous other professionals.[17] Consistent with the Carkhuff Approach, the initial stage, *telling*, involved a didactic presentation of material. This was followed by *showing* in which the presenter used videos and live role plays to demonstrate concepts and techniques. In this study, these 2 stages were conducted both in the large group of 80-100 participants and then in small groups of about 12. The *doing* stage, which occurred in the smaller group, involved exercises where participants practiced what they heard and watched. Stage four, *repeating*, involved a series of exercises of progressively complex techniques. Each exercise focused primarily on one concept with subsequent exercises building on what had been learned to gradually increase in complexity. *Applying* occurred when the participants used what they learned in the training in their jobs treating substance abusing clients.

Baumgarten and Roffers cautioned that learners who adhered to counseling theories with disparate principles to the new approach may respond to training with the wholesale rejection of the new approach.[17] To address such a problem, they suggested that learners engage in reflection as a means to accommodate aspects of the new approach that are compatible with their personal philosophy of treatment. In the current study, some participants were expected to embrace techniques inconsistent with MET such as confrontation or labeling. In response, reflective exercises were infused throughout the training program. One of the exercises even directly addressed participants' reactions to using MET. Also, to address issues relating to the client populations of the study participants (i.e., adolescent and post- or currently-incarcerated individuals) the training infused case material with problems specific to these populations.

We conducted 2 trainings, attended by 80-110 participants each, which consisted of a 2-day conference followed a month later by a 4-hour booster. In the 2-day training, basic concepts and techniques were presented and demonstrated through didactic presentation, role plays and videos. This information was then reinforced through further didactic instruction and practiced through exercises in smaller groups of about 10-15 participants. One month later, participants returned for a 4-hour booster training session during which they addressed the facilitators and barriers of implementing MET in the work setting, practiced MET techniques covered during the conference, and took part in an interactive exercise on cultural competency. The booster training also served to correct treatment drift, in which the principles and techniques learned sometimes change over time and become different from the original technology taught.[10] The benefits of brief follow-up training is supported in the literature.[18]

Consistency of the small group sessions in the 2-day conference was maintained with over 40 hours of training for MET trainers which included a 2-day private training by Dr. Teresa Moyers, an MET expert and trainer from the Motivational Interviewing Network of Trainers (MINT). Additional training of trainers was facilitated by an in-house MET expert. That expert along with 14 other professionals led the small groups. Two trainers were assigned to co-lead each small group, of which at least one had clinical psychotherapy experience. All small-group trainers followed an in-house training manual,[19] and completed a checklist of training tasks to ensure consistency. An MET treatment manual[20] was provided to all participants. This manual was a revision of the MET manual used in the MATCH study[6] and included supplements on MET with post or currently-incarcerated substance-involved offenders and substance-involved adolescents. These supplements were developed based on a literature review and input from provider and client focus groups. Thus, training reliability and integrity were supported through extensive training of trainers sessions, assigning two trainers for each small group of participants, using a training manual, monitoring using a checklist of specific training activities, and distributing an MET manual for participants.

Design

A repeated measures design was used to assess the effect of MET training on participant knowledge, attitudes, and behaviors. There were three arms to the analysis: immediate training, delayed training, and no training. Those in the delayed condition received training 4 months after the immediate condition, and those in the no training condition could not or chose not to attend training. Subjects completed surveys at 3 timepoints separated by 4 months. Those in the immediate condition received training between the T1 and T2 surveys, whereas those in the delayed condition received training between the T2 and T3 surveys. Originally, random assignment to the immediate and delayed treatment groups was employed. However, due to low adherence to assignment (49%) based primarily on participants not showing for training the randomization scheme was discarded and the analysis was conducted as-trained rather than intent-to-train. No statistically significant T1 differences were found in demographic or outcome variables when comparing trained versus not trained or when comparing all three conditions.

RESULTS

Two hundred ninety individuals representing more than 40 agencies returned at least one survey. Twenty-three individuals did not meet inclusion criteria for the study and were removed from this analysis. Of the 267 eligible individuals, 74 (28%) attended the immediate training intervention, 98 (37%) attended the delayed training, and 95 (36%) did not attend the training. Two-thirds (68%) of the sample were female, 60% were African-American, and slightly over half (52%) had a master's degree. The median age was 42 years ($SD = 11.3$) and a little over half (52%) had 5 or more years of addictions counseling experience. About half (53%) came from agencies with fewer than 25 employees, whereas 20% treated adolescents, 54% treated currently- or post-incarcerated adults, and 26% treated both groups.

To accommodate the unbalanced, repeated measures design of this study, generalized estimating equations (GEE) models[21] were used to assess the impact of the training for each of the five outcome variables. Factors in the analysis included group (3 levels: immediate, delayed and no training conditions) and time (3 levels), where time was the repeated measure. A significant group by time interaction suggested that the outcomes for each group changed at different rates over time. These effects were pursued by analyzing subsets of groups and times. All group by time interactions were significant at $p < .001$, except for MET Techniques, which was significant at $p < .01$ (see Table 1). Sub-analyses of the immediate treatment effect (trained vs. not trained, pre- and post-training) indicate that all group by time interactions were significant at

TABLE 1. Training Effect Over Time for MET Knowledge, Attitudes, and Behaviors (Generalized Estimating Equations)

| Outcome Variable | Descriptive Statistics | | | | | | χ^2 statistics | | |
| | Time 1 | | Time 2 | | Time 3 | | | | |
Condition	M (SD)[1]	n	M (SD)	n	M (SD)	n	Group	Time	Group × Time
Knowledge							39.4**	112.3**	89.7**
Immediate	4.7 (3.5)	73	8.4 (2.1)	64	8.5 (1.8)	52			
Delayed	4.8 (3.4)	97	5.4 (3.5)	87	8.2 (2.4)	60			
No Training	3.9 (3.2)	92	4.4 (3.5)	46	4.2 (3.4)	24			
Attitudes							17.5**	69.7**	38.1**
Immediate	4.0 (0.6)	73	4.4 (0.6)	66	4.4 (0.6)	52			
Delayed	3.9 (0.7)	97	3.9 (0.6)	87	4.2 (0.6)	60			
No training	3.8 (0.6)	95	3.9 (0.7)	46	3.8 (0.8)	24			
Percent MET Used							102.7**	42.9**	52.5**
Immediate	1.0 (1.3)	72	2.6 (1.2)	64	2.8 (1.1)	52			
Delayed	1.0 (1.2)	92	1.4 (1.4)	84	2.3 (1.2)	60			
No Training	0.9 (1.2)	93	1.1 (1.3)	44	1.1 (1.2)	23			
MET Techniques							3.2**	15.5**	16.8*
Immediate	2.5 (0.6)	69	2.8 (0.6)	63	2.8 (0.8)	52			
Delayed	2.5 (0.7)	90	2.5 (0.8)	85	2.7 (0.8)	58			
No Training	2.5 (0.7)	91	2.5 (0.7)	43	2.5 (0.6)	24			
Vignette Responses							17.5**	69.7**	38.1**
Immediate	1.7 (0.7)	65	2.3 (0.7)	60	2.3 (0.7)	46			
Delayed	1.7 (0.7)	83	2.0 (0.7)	75	2.4 (0.6)	53			
No Training	1.6 (0.7)	82	1.8 (0.7)	40	1.7 (0.7)	19			

* $p < 0.01$; ** $p < 0.001$
[1] M(SD) = mean (standard deviation)

$p < 0.01$ except behaviors which were significant at $p = 0.05$ (data not shown).

For the maintenance effect (looking at T2 to T3 effects for the immediate group), none of the group by time interactions were significant reflecting no change for any of the outcome variables.

The pattern indicating improvement and maintenance is for the immediate group to increase between T1 and T2 (during which they are trained) and for the delayed and no training group to show no change. Then, between T2 and T3 the delayed group, which is trained during that time period, should increase to the same level as the immediate group, the immediate group should maintain its level of change at a higher plateau, the no training group should show no change. This pattern is reflected in all of the outcome variables except the delayed group showed slight pre-training increases (i.e., between T1 and T2) for Percent MET Used and Vignette Responses.

When reviewing the magnitude of change from before until after training (T1-T2 for the immediate group and T2-T3 for the delayed group), there are some differences with regard to the clinical relevance of the improvement. Notable improvement was demonstrated for Knowledge (an immediate and delayed condition average increase of about 70% correct answers), Percent MET Used (an increase from 1-25% to approximately 26-50% for the delayed group and between 26-50% and 51-75% for the immediate group), and Vignette Responses (a 25% increase). More modest improvement was evident for Attitudes (.3 [delayed] to .4 [immediate] improvement on a 5-point scale) and MET Techniques (.2 [delayed] to .3 [immediate] improvement on a 5-point scale).

DISCUSSION

The results of this study suggest that a brief MET training, based on the Carkhuff Approach, effectively increases MET knowledge, attitudes, and behaviors, and there is indication that the changes are maintained over a 4-month period. Despite the statistically significant findings, Attitudes and MET Techniques showed only modest improvement. The modest Attitude changes may be due to the fact that the sample chose to participate in the training, they already held positive attitudes about MET (about 1 point below the maximum score), and they consequently had limited opportunity for improvement. With regard to MET techniques, Miller and Mount report that although trained participants increased MET behaviors (i.e., techniques), they also retained MET inconsistent behaviors.[10] In view of these findings, counselors may attenuate improvement in MET techniques through retaining MET inconsistent behaviors, which may explain the unimpressive changes.

Knowledge, Percent MET Used, and Vignette responses all showed notable improvements, yet changes in Percent MET Used may be suspect. Miller and Mount reported in their study that counselors' self-reports of change were more optimistic than their actual behavioral changes demonstrated, suggesting that the change reflected in this measure may not accurately reflect behavioral change.[10] The remaining behavior score, Vignette responses, showed less pronounced changes than Knowledge, presumably because behavior is more difficult to change and requires more intense training for large improvement. This is supported by Miller et al. and Sholomskas et al.'s studies in which various types of supervision were employed to supplement workshops resulting in large behavior improvement.[4,15] The 4-hour booster session employed in the current study may facilitate and maintained behavioral change; however, ongoing supervision appears to amplify behavioral gains.

Of the outcome variables used in this study, Vignette Responses most accurately evaluates the adoption of MET and therefore provides the most compelling evidence that change occurred in the counselors' behavior. This is because in response to a case vignette, respondents were asked to write what they would say "as if it were a real counseling session." High scores on this measure would require basic MET knowledge (which is supported by notable improvement on this scale), an ability to use MET techniques, positive attitudes, and a plan to use MET in therapy. Therefore, the size and statistical significance of the improvement along with the maintenance of that improvement suggest that the training protocol facilitates the adoption of MET. Thus, Knowledge, Percent MET Used, and Vignette Responses showed notable changes that appeared to be clinically relevant, whereas Attitudes and MET Techniques showed less meaningful improvement.

The lack of more robust changes may be due to a number of factors. Participants may have increased MET behaviors and initiated adoption as a result of the training, although they were not yet proficient at this approach and required further training.[10] Anecdotally, participants who adhered to the disease model, which constituted slightly over one-quarter of our sample, sometimes found the MET approach to be contrary to their counseling philosophy and chose not use it in their practice. This too may have attenuated improvement.

It is interesting to note that the delayed condition showed some improvement from T1 to T2 both in the Vignette Responses and Percent MET Used. It is possible that the delayed group, in anticipation of the training they would receive, pursued MET skills both through their agencies where colleagues in the immediate group shared information, and through personal study.

Limitations

One limitation of this study was the restricted capacity of the outcome variables, which were all self-report, to measure in vivo counselor-client behaviors. As suggested earlier, the strongest outcome variable in this study was the written response to the case vignettes. Unfortunately, a written response did not capture the full range of responses a counselor could provide with actual clients, particularly in situations that were stressful, frustrating, or antagonistic. Furthermore, Vignette Responses were only intended to elicit one type of counselor-client interaction–how the counselor handled client ambivalence. There are a host of other interactions in which an MET-consistent response may be more or less challenging to provide. Additionally, MET requires knowledge and behaviors that are sustained over the course of a counseling session, and the entire course of therapy, with different dynamics arising over time. Clearly, the written response could not capture this complexity in therapeutic interaction. It was also likely that response bias was present. Respondents may have wished to demonstrate improvement in MET behaviors, even if they did not actually employ such techniques with their clients. To compensate for these limitations, the variables used in this study were intended to be comprehensive, covering knowledge, attitudes, and three different measures of behavior.

Another limitation relating to measurement was the relatively low reliability scores for some of the instruments. Retest reliability for four of the measures ranged from .48 to .69, and the internal consistency for one of the measures was at $\alpha = .65$. Retest scores may have been depressed due to a learning effect and the extended time between testings. For example, participants in the retest analysis may have improved their outcome scores between T1 and T2 as a result of colleagues in the immediate condition (not in the retest analysis) discussing their application of MET in consultation meetings or supervision. This speculation is supported by T1-T2 improvement in most delayed and no training condition scores (see Table 1). The 4-month interval between testings probably also reduced the retest scores.

A potential limitation is transferability of the training program, which may pose some challenges. The training was successful in inducing a diverse group of counselors from southern Louisiana serving substance-involved adolescents and/or incarcerated/post-incarcerated substance-involved offenders to adopt MET in their practices. Although the training may be transferable to a broad range of counselors with regard to race, gender, work environment, and education, care would need to be taken when adapting the training to other cultural groups of clients, or with treatment approaches other than MET. Another potential barrier to transferability is that trainers required considerable knowledge about MET and how to train others in this approach. Consequently, one would need the resources to acquire adequate training from quality organizations such as the Motivational Interviewing Network of Trainers (MINT).

A limitation in the design of this study is that 4 months was a short time to illustrate maintenance of adoption. The authors chose to limit the follow-up period to 4 month in order to minimize potential attrition of participants and related confounds that might result from a longer follow-up period.

A further limitation was attrition associated with randomization, and uneven attrition over time across the 3 conditions. Attrition problems in randomization prevented adherence to a controlled experimental design. Nevertheless, Time 1 comparisons across the immediate, delayed and no training groups suggested that the samples were comparable. Rates of T1-T3 attrition differed for the immediate (29%) and delayed (38%) versus the no training (74%) conditions (see Knowledge statistics in Table 1). Yet, relatively similar T2 means across all variables between the delayed and no training group, and between the T2 and T3 no training group scores suggested that the effects were not due primarily to differential attrition.

Conclusions

Given the results and limitations, there remains support suggesting that a brief Carkhuff-based MET training protocol can facilitate the adoption of MET. The changes demonstrated by study participants represent the beginning of a training process that, if the trainee chooses to continue, can lead to proficient MET behaviors. Miller and Mount caution that the workshop may instigate a false sense of MI proficiency which could lead to avoiding further training opportunities.[10] Anecdotally, we have not experienced resistance to further training. Rather, we witnessed strong interest for workshops we provided focusing on basic

MET behaviors, MET with groups, advanced MET, and ongoing MET supervision training, all of which have been well attended. The expansion of counselors who employ MET within agencies will likely enhance proficiency and heighten interest in further training. Given Miller and Mount's warning, it would be prudent to introduce workshops on beginning MET behaviors as such, and to educate attendees about the necessity for further training if they desire proficiency. Furthermore, ongoing supervision appears to amplify and maintain gains.[4,15] It is unlikely that post-degree professionals will change their major method of acquiring counseling skills–the workshop. Consequently, workshop quality needs careful scrutiny, evaluation, and enhancement. Researchers need to investigate who responds best to what types of workshops, how to attract attendees to more intensive ongoing trainings, and new methods to heighten learning that occurs in these workshops.

AUTHORS NOTE

The authors would like to acknowledge the contributions of Katherine Bevans, Rebecca Chaisson, Mary Craighead, Evelyn Harrell, Patricia Keller, John King, Reginald Parquet, Rena Smith, Melanie Steen-Sighinolfi, Angela Wood, and Merlin Young.

This research was supported by the Center for Substance Abuse Treatment, and Substance Abuse and Mental Health Services Administration (Contract No. 5 UD1 TI12906).

REFERENCES

1. McLellan AT. Technology transfer and the treatment of addiction: What can research offer practice? J Subst Abuse Treat. 2002; 22:169-170.

2. Dansereau DF, Dees SM. Mapping training: The transfer of a cognitive technology for improving counseling. J Subst Abuse Treat. 2002; 22:219-230.

3. CSAT. The change book: A blueprint for technology transfer. Kansas City: Addiction Technology Transfer Center National Office, 2000.

4. Sholomskas DE, Syracuse-Siewert G, Rounsaville, BJ, Ball, SA, Nuro, KF, Carroll KM. We don't train in vain: A controlled trial of three strategies of training clinicians in cognitive-behavioral therapy. J Consult Clin Psychol. 2005; 73:106-115.

5. Simpson DD. A conceptual framework for transferring research to practice. 2002; J Subst Abuse Treat, 24:171-182.

6. Miller WR, Zweben A, DiClemente CC, Rychtarik RG. Motivational Enhancement Therapy Manual: Project MATCH Monograph Series Volume 2. Rockville, MD: NIH, 1997.

7. Rollnick S, Miller WR. What is motivational interviewing? Behav Cognit Psychother. 1995; 23:325-334.

8. Miller WR, Rollnick S. Motivational interviewing: Preparing people for change (2nd ed.). New York: The Guilford Press, 2002.

9. Doherty Y, Hall D, James PT, Roberts SH, Simpson J. Change counseling in diabetes: The development of a training programme for the diabetes team. Patient Educ Couns. 2000; 40:263-278.

10. Miller WR, Mount KA. A small study of training in motivational interviewing: Does one workshop change clinician and client behavior? Behav Cognit Psychother. 2001; 29:457-471.

11. Gregoire TK. Assessing the benefits and increasing the utility of addiction training for public child welfare workers: A pilot study. Child Welfare. 1994; 73(1):69-81.

12. Rivers PC, Sarata BPV, Book T. Effect of an alcoholism workshop on attitudes, job satisfaction and job performance of secretaries. Q J Stud Alcohol. 1974; 35:1382-1388.

13. Crits-Christoph P, Siqueland L, Chittams J, et al. Training in cognitive, supportive-expressive, and drug counseling therapies for cocaine dependence. J Consult Clin Psychol. 1998; 66:484-492.

14. Rubel EC, Sobell LC, Miller WR. Do continuing education workshops improve participants' skills? Effects of a motivational interviewing workshop on substance abuse counselors' skills and knowledge. Behav Therapist. 2000; 23(4):73-77, 90.

15. Miller WR, Yahne CE, Moyers TB, Martinez J, Pirritano M. A randomized trial of methods to help clinicians learn Motivational Interviewing. J Consult Clin Psychol. 2004; 72:1050-1062.

16. Shafer MS, Rhode R, Chong J. Utilizing distance education to promote the transfer of motivational interviewing skills among behavioral health professionals. J Subst Abuse Treat. 2004; 26(2):141-148.

17. Baumgarten E, Roffers T. Implementing and expanding on Carkhuff's Training Technology. J Cons Dev. 2003; 81(3):285-292.

18. Ball K, Berch D, Helmers KF, et al. Effects of cognitive training interventions with older adults: A randomized controlled trial. JAMA. 2002; 288:2271-2281.

19. Toriello PJ. Motivational Enhancement Therapy for substance involved individuals: Facilitators' manual for breakout sessions. Unpublished manuscript, 2002.

20. New Orleans Practice Improvement Collaborative (NOPIC) Motivational Enhancement Therapy with substance-involved individuals: A clinical research guide for counselors working with substance-involved individuals. Unpublished manuscript, 2002.

21. Hanley JA, Negassa A, Edwardes MD, Forrester JE. Statistical analysis of correlated data using Generalized Estimating Equations: An orientation. Am J Epidemiol. 2003; 157(4):364-375.

Substance Abuse Counseling: What Is Treatment as Usual?

Michele J. Eliason, PhD
Stephan Arndt, PhD
Arthur Schut, MS

SUMMARY. As the field begins to explore methods of introducing evidence-based practices to substance abuse treatment agencies, there is a need to determine the extent to which evidence based practices are already being used. We developed a self-report instrument to measure treatment philosophies and everyday practices, and surveyed 197 treatment counselors about their overall treatment philosophies, what practices they had been trained to use, and what specific techniques and principles they used in their everyday practice. The instrument focused on use of six treatment philosophies often reported to be used in substance abuse treatment settings: Cognitive Behavioral, Contingency Management-Behavioral, Motivational Enhancement, 12 step, Psychodynamic-Insight Oriented, and Therapeutic Community. The results showed very little correspondence between the treatment philosophies

Michele J. Eliason is Associate Professor, and Stephan Arndt is Professor, University of Iowa.

Arthur Schut is Executive Director, Mid-Eastern Council on Chemical Abuse.

Address correspondence to: Michele J. Eliason, 372 NB, College of Nursing, University of Iowa, Iowa City, IA 52242 (E-mail: mickey-eliason@uiowa.edu).

This research was supported by a grant from the Center for Substance Abuse Treatment, Practice Improvement Collaborative, Grant # 5 UD1 TI12632-02.

[Haworth co-indexing entry note]: "Substance Abuse Counseling: What Is Treatment as Usual?" Eliason, Michele J., Stephan Arndt, and Arthur Schut. Co-published simultaneously in *Journal of Addictive Diseases* (The Haworth Medical Press, an imprint of The Haworth Press, Inc.) Vol. 24, Supplement No. 1, 2005, pp. 33-51; and: *Implementing Evidence-Based Practices for Treatment of Alcohol and Drug Disorders* (ed: Eldon Edmundson, Jr., and Dennis McCarty) The Haworth Medical Press, an imprint of The Haworth Press, Inc., 2005, pp. 33-51. Single or multiple copies of this article are available for a fee from The Haworth Document Delivery Service [1-800-HAWORTH, 9:00 a.m. - 5:00 p.m. (EST). E-mail address: docdelivery@haworthpress.com].

that counselors said they used and the actual techniques or tools they reported using in daily practice. Most counselors endorsed use of more than one theoretical approach to treatment. Implications of these findings for the field are discussed. *[Article copies available for a fee from The Haworth Document Delivery Service: 1-800-HAWORTH. E-mail address: <docdelivery@haworthpress.com> Website: <http://www.HaworthPress.com>* © *2005 by The Haworth Press, Inc. All rights reserved.]*

KEYWORDS. Treatment philosophies, evidenced-based practices

As substance abuse counseling evolves from a self-help movement into a profession, and as research on treatment effectiveness increases, there is a critical need to examine the practices that are currently used in the field. In the past ten years, there has been a growing body of biological, psychological, and socio-cultural research on substance abuse, but the findings of this research have not yet been consistently applied to the field.[1] Randomized clinical trials of substance abuse treatments have been conducted (for example, Project Match[2]), the National Institute on Drug Abuse (NIDA) has formally initiated a Clinical Trials Network to understand which treatments work and how they work, and the Center for Substance Abuse Treatment (CSAT) has several projects that explore how to apply evidence-based practices to the field.

Most experimental research compares some new approach to "treatment as usual" but rarely specifies what is meant by treatment as usual. In a field as diverse as substance abuse treatment, where training ranges from one's personal experiences with recovery to PhD's in addiction studies, how do we characterize typical substance abuse treatment? There has been surprisingly little empirical research on what constitutes treatment as usual. A number of studies have examined beliefs about one treatment modality or focused on one clinician or client characteristic.[3-7] The few studies that have a broader focus were conducted outside of the United States.[8,9]

Forman et al.[10] surveyed 317 substance abuse treatment providers' beliefs about addiction treatment. Contrary to research findings that confrontational methods are harmful, 46% of the participants believed that confrontation should be used more often, and 36% agreed that noncompliant clients should be discharged. These counselors did not show strong support for use of medications, but were quite supportive of using other research-based approaches.

Ogborne et al.[11] surveyed over 2000 counselors in Canada about specific treatment processes such as 12 step programming, drug and alcohol education, family systems approaches and rehabilitation approaches. The questionnaire items factored into four groups which the authors labeled as Cognitive-Behavioral, Disease Model, Insight-Behavioral, and Medication factors. However, only 2% of respondents clearly endorsed only one of these factors. The highest endorsement of items was for the cognitive behavioral factor, including focusing on cognitions, teaching coping skills, and engaging in relapse prevention activities. Ratings of medication use were quite low and often negative. The third factor, Insight-Behavioral, was a combination of psychodynamic therapy and behavioral approaches. The authors suggested that this combination warrants further study as it might reveal some overlap between psychodynamic and conditioning perspectives, which on the surface appear to be oppositional approaches. For example, automatic processes as conceptualized by behavioral approaches might be interpreted as unconscious processes in psychodynamic theory–thus the same construct or concept might be interpreted from different perspectives. Scores on the Disease Model scale were negatively correlated with scores on the medication scale, possibly reflecting the commonly held misconception that 12 step approaches oppose the use of medications.

Ball et al.[4] surveyed 66 counselors who had volunteered to participate in a clinical trial of motivational interviewing. Counselors said that they "very much" endorsed a 12 step/disease model (41%), relapse prevention/Cognitive Behavioral Therapy model (36%), reality therapy (17%), and motivational interviewing (14%). Few counselors reported use of only one theoretical perspective.

In conclusion, researchers may be clear on what they mean by Twelve Step, Motivational Enhancement, Cognitive-Behavioral, and other treatment philosophies, but there is less evidence that front-line counselors, who often have very little formal training, implement evidence-based therapy approaches. Ideally, direct observation studies would be used to determine what counselors actually do, but there is considerable expense and the risk of observer bias in this approach. This preliminary, descriptive study used a self-report format to determine if there is a relationship between the treatment philosophies that counselors say they use, and the actual daily practices they say they use. If counselors understand and endorse a particular theoretical framework, their practice should be somewhat consistent with that orientation. This information may be useful in designing more sophisticated observational studies in the future, and will also prove useful as a first step in identifying what is meant by "treatment as usual."

METHOD

Instrument

An instrument was developed specifically for use in the study when the literature review did not reveal any existing instruments. The questionnaire has three main components: assessment of treatment philosophies; assessment of specific practices and principles; and demographic/personal information.

Treatment Philosophies

The instrument assessed the degree to which treatment providers were using the principles or approaches of the major evidence based practices. Thus, we first assembled a list of widely used philosophical approaches, which included 12 step, motivational enhancement, cognitive-behavioral, contingency management-behavioral, psychodynamic-insight-oriented, and therapeutic community approaches. Although few counselors in our region are trained to be psychodynamic therapists, concepts drawn from psychoanalysis/Freudian theory are often reported. We did not consider pharmacological treatment of addictions because medications are not used widely in community based treatment programs in our region, and when used, are used in conjunction with some sort of behavioral therapy. A series of questions examined the counselor's theoretical approach to substance abuse counseling. Respondents were asked to indicate if they had training in each of the six approaches, which of the approaches they felt competent to carry out, which approaches characterized their own usual practice, and which approaches characterized their agency as a whole.

Everyday Practices (Fidelity Scales)

Based on a review of the literature of the six theoretical approaches, we selected five to six major principles or techniques that are considered the unique features of the approach. We also reviewed the Center for Substance Abuse Treatment's Technical Assistance Publication on counselor competency[12] and generated items that represent basic counselor competencies regardless of theoretical approach (e.g., empathy, culturally-specific practice, positive regard for clients). Finally, we included items on practices that are reportedly used in treatment that are not strictly within a specific theoretical framework, such as use of Native American spirituality concepts, decreasing family "enabling" behaviors, and anger management training. The result was a scale of 51 items that included six fidelity scales related to the six major theoretical approaches and one miscellaneous factor including the basic counselor competencies and isolated techniques. Items related to the specific treatment approaches were randomly placed in the scale along with the counselor competencies and other items. Respondents were asked to indicate if they never, rarely, sometimes, or often used each principle or technique.

Demographic/Personal Information

Demographic information included type of work setting (residential, outpatient, other and correctional, community or hospital/institution), urban/rural setting, roles in the agency, and formal education (and whether that education was in substance abuse counseling, another counseling field, or a non-counseling field). We also asked how many hours per week they spend in client assessment, group treatment, individual treatment, paperwork, administration, updating skills, and "putting out fires." Another item addressed the percentage of clients that respondents thought were truly motivated to change and the percent of clients that they thought were successful in achieving long-term sobriety.

Since the project stemmed from a CSAT funded project, we were also interested in how often respondents used materials generated from CSAT (TIPS and TAPS) in their practice (never, rarely, sometimes, often), and if they used them, how useful they found them to be. We also included an open-ended question, "What manuals, books, guides, or other resource materials do you use the most often to guide your own practice?"

The final section of the questionnaire included personal information, including sex, age, years worked as a substance abuse counselor, race/ethnicity, recovery status, and job stress.

Sample

Participants were recruited in two ways. Surveys were distributed at a statewide annual conference on substance abuse (200 surveys were

distributed and 89 were returned). Secondly, we asked program directors of three community based treatment agencies in eastern Iowa to
distribute questionnaires to their line staff (141 distributed and 107 returned). Overall, 341 surveys were distributed and 197 returned for a response rate of 57%. The respondents were predominantly female (77%),
white (91%), and well-educated. Over one-third (37%) reported that
they had completed formal coursework in substance abuse counseling,
whereas 60% had formal education in other counseling fields. Most
(71%) worked in community based treatment organizations and identified their roles as addiction counselors (79%), whereas 23% worked in
community corrections or prison-based treatment programs, and 7%
worked in hospital-based programs. Less than 20% (18%) indicated
that they were clinical supervisors. Over half worked with a combination of urban and rural clients, although nearly 30% served only rural
clients, and 62% worked only in outpatient treatment programs. They
had worked in the substance abuse field for an average of 7.2 years
(SD = 6.3) with a range of two months to 39 years. About one-fourth of
the sample (27%) had worked as counselors for two years or less.
Slightly over one-third (36%) reported that they were in recovery themselves, and had been for 2 to 30 years (mean of 15.4 years, SD = 6.4).
The majority of the respondents thought that most of their clients were
not motivated to change (64%) and most clients would not achieve
long-term sobriety (76%).

Counselors in this study spent much of their typical week doing paperwork related to clients (a mean of 10.6 hours, SD = 9.1), followed by
individual treatment (mean of 9.6 hours, SD = 7.4), client assessment
(mean of 5.4 hours, SD = 5.5), group treatment (mean of 5.4 hours, SD =
5.3), administrative duties or supervision (mean of 4.8 hours, SD = 11.2),
"putting out fires" (mean of 3.0 hours, SD = 5.6), and finally, updating
their skills and preparing for client work (mean of 3.0 hours, SD = 3.0).

RESULTS

Counselor Everyday Activities and Treatment Philosophies

The 51 items assessing the counselor's use of activities, principles, or
techniques were categorized according to the literature review of the six
treatment models under study: 12 step, cognitive behavioral, therapeutic
community, contingency management-behavioral, motivational enhancement, and psychodynamic-insight. The items within each theoretical

framework were summed to create a fidelity scale score. As a check for internal consistency, the correlation of each item was assessed against its own scale and against the other scales. All items except for one, showed the highest correlation with its own scale relative to the other scales. That item, "Avoiding confrontation and breaking down denial or defense mechanisms until a strong working alliance has been built with the client" was originally thought to contribute to the psychodynamic scale, but lowered the Cronbach's alpha coefficient for this scale. Thus, this item was dropped.

Table 1 shows the internal consistency estimates for each of the six theoretical approach fidelity scales. The fidelity scales show only moderate internal consistency, with none of the scales producing an alpha coefficient higher than 0.70. The table also shows the number of respondents who said that they used the approach/principle in their usual practice. Nearly three-fourths of counselors (73%) said that they used more than one approach. The most common approach was Cognitive Behavioral with 81% endorsement, followed by motivational enhancement (51%) and 12 step approaches (47%). Reflecting the relatively high number of counselors from correctional settings, one in four reported using a therapeutic community approach. Eight percent of respondents indicated "other" and listed practices such as family systems, existential, reality therapy, brief therapy, and person-centered approaches.

Correlations among the scales indicated a fair amount of overlap in the treatment model approaches. The 12 step model showed considerable overlap with the Behavioral and Psychodynamic models. For example, of the 11 counselors who claimed that they often helped "clients see substance abuse as a fixation to an earlier stage of development," 8

TABLE 1. Fidelity Scales: Internal consistency and respondent endorsement

Scale	# of items	Cronbach's alpha	% respondent endorsement
12 step	6	0.68	47
Cognitive behavioral	7	0.64	81
Therapeutic community	4	0.67	24
Behavioral	4	0.521	10
Motivational enhancement	9	0.69	51
Psychodynamic	4	0.65	8

of these (73%) said that they used a 12 step model for treatment. On the other hand, 12 step practices were relatively independent (although marginally correlated) with motivational enhancement techniques. Table 2 shows the intercorrelations among the practice model fidelity scales. All of the correlations shown in Table 2 are higher when corrected for attenuation from unreliability.

Since counselors typically reported that they used more than one approach in their usual practice, Table 3 shows the associations among the approaches. The patterns among the approaches are fairly weak, however, some interesting patterns were noted. For example, counselors who ascribed to a 12 step model said that they did not use motivational enhancement whereas counselors who ascribed to motivational enhancement were likely to report that they also used therapeutic commu-

TABLE 2. Pearson r correlations among the model fidelity scales

	12 step	Cog Beh	TC	Beh	Mot Enh	Psychodynamic
12 step	1.00	0.40	0.46	0.51	0.17	0.55
Cog Beh	0.40	1.00	0.53	0.50	0.52	0.40
TC	0.46	0.53	1.00	0.49	0.47	0.38
Beh	0.51	0.50	0.49	1.00	0.35	0.30
Mot Enh	0.17	0.52	0.47	0.35	1.00	0.30
Psycho	0.55	0.40	0.38	0.30	0.30	1.00

95% confidence intervals are roughly = ±0.13, df = 195. All correlations are significant at p < .001 except for motivational enhancement and 12 step, which had a p value of 0.02.

TABLE 3. Correlations (Kendall's tau) among the approaches that counselors endorsed as their usual practices

	12 step	Cog Beh	Mot Enh	Beh	TC	Psychodynamic
12 step	1.00	0.01	−.15	0.09	0.14	−0.003
Cog Beh	0.01	1.00	−0.01	0.16 *	0.09	0.14
Mot Enh	0.15*	−0.01	1.00	0.13	0.17*	0.02
Beh	0.09	0.16*	0.13	1.00	0.25*	0.16*
TC	0.14	0.09	0.17*	0.25**	1.00	0.06
Psycho	−0.003	0.14	0.02	0.16*	0.06	1.00

* p > .05,   ** p < .01.

nity techniques. Counselors who ascribed to behavioral methods also tended to use therapeutic community techniques.

The next comparison examined the practices that counselors said typified their usual practice as compared to what they actually reported doing as measured by the fidelity scales. Table 4 shows the relationships between stated treatment philosophy, and clusters of principles/ techniques that make up those practices.

Counselors who reported that they used a 12 step approach in their usual practice also tended to score significantly on the 12 step fidelity model. This is the highest correlation in the table, suggesting less than 13% (0.35^2) of the variance on the fidelity scale measuring the activities, principles, and techniques of a 12 step approach. Similarly, there was a slight tendency for counselors who reported that they used a cognitive behavioral approach in their usual practice to score higher on the cognitive behavioral fidelity scale. Counselors who said they used behavioral, therapeutic community, 12 step, and psychodynamic models tended to use several psychodynamic principles and techniques. Nonparametric correlations produced nearly identical results. Since counselors ascribed to more than one model in their usual practice, the low correlations might be due to the mixed nature of counselor approaches. To assess this possibility, we reconstructed the correlations of each usual model with the scales controlling for the other models that counselors endorsed as their usual practice. If multiple approaches tend to reduce the correlations, the partial correlations should be increased particularly for the relevant scale-approach combination (e.g., 12 step approach with the 12 step fidelity scale). However, the correlations

TABLE 4. Correlations between stated usual practice and fidelity scales

Usual Practice	12 step	Cog Beh	TC	Beh	Mot Enh	Psycho
12 step	0.35 **	0.01	0.02	0.1	−0.10	0.17 *
Cog Beh	0.06	0.18 *	0.05	0.14	0.06	0.09
Mot Enh	−0.02	0.23 **	0.07	0.10	0.21 **	−0.01
Beh	0.12	0.19 **	0.06	0.07	0.11	0.24 **
TC	0.25 **	0.23 **	0.26 **	0.26 **	0.14	0.19 **
Psycho	−0.01	0.04	−0.06	−0.09	0.06	0.15 *
Other	0.01	0.07	0.05	0.00	0.03	0.08

* p < .05, ** p < .01.

were virtually identical to those shown in Table 4. We also conducted analyses controlling for the correlations between scales with essentially identical results.

Factor Analysis Attempts

Several attempts were made at factor analyzing these items. None of the exploratory factor solutions (principal components, principal axis, or alpha) reproduced the fidelity scales. The sample principal components analysis provided ten factors with eigenvalues greater than one. Inspection of the scree plot, however, suggested seven or eight factors accounting for 53% and 56% of the variance, respectively. Using the seven factor solution and varimax rotation, the first factor was characterized by items suggesting a psychodynamic orientation. These items included "fostering exploration of early childhood experiences" (item #42, loading = 0.70) and "using tools such as dream analysis and free association to uncover unconscious material" (item #5, loading = 0.61). However two items indicative of 12 step models also showed high loadings on this factor: "helping clients discover their higher power" (item #41, loading = 0.62) and "encouraging clients to admit they are powerless over substances" (item #6, loading = 0.61). The second factor's three highest loading items dealt with involvement of peers in the recovery process (items 4, 7, and 37). These items included techniques thought to be part of a 12 step model (finding a sponsor and peer help) as well as the therapeutic community model (peer self governance and accountability). The other factors also produced hybrid item constellations.

In addition to the exploratory analyses, a multiple group factor analysis was done.[13,14] The factors were defined by the a priori categorization of the six fidelity scales. The six predefined factors (i.e., fidelity scales) accounted for only 41.5% of the variance. Item communalities produced fairly poor results with only three items showing communality greater than 0.50. This indicates that for the overwhelming majority of items, the factor solution accounted for less than 50% of the item's variance. Similar results appeared for oblique and orthogonal solutions.

What Counselors Actually Do

Table 5 shows the individual items that make up the fidelity scales, displays mean scores, and shows the percent of respondents who reported that they used the principle/technique "often." Many of the items

TABLE 5. Individual items composing the fidelity scales

Principle/technique	Fidelity Scale	Mean (SD)	% who use it often
1. Breaking down a client's denial through confrontation	TC	2.84 (0.88)	25
2. Helping clients recognize that behavior is learned, thus bad behavior can be unlearned	CB	3.62 (0.64)	69
3. Educating clients on the disease model of addiction	12	3.48 (0.77)	62
4. Recruiting peers to help each other maintain sobriety	12	3.23 (0.91)	49
5. Using tools such as dream analysis and free association to get at unconscious material	Freud	1.55 (0.77)	3
6. Encouraging clients to admit they are powerless over substances	12	3.01 (0.98)	39
7. Using peers as a therapeutic tool to increase accountability	TC	3.39 (0.79)	54
8. Listening more than talking	ME	3.72 (0.46)	73
9. Teaching clients how to identify their feelings and express them appropriately	CB	3.82 (0.46)	85
10. Helping clients to recognize faulty thinking patterns	CB	3.83 (0.44)	86
11. Helping clients see substance abuse as a fixation to an earlier stage of development	Freud	2.00 (0.95)	6
12. Using activities that help clients modify their thinking	CB	3.51 (0.68)	59
13. Educating clients on signs and symptoms of relapse/lapse and help them identify triggers	CC	3.90 (0.33)	91
14. Avoiding arguments with clients	ME	3.62 (0.70)	73
15. Working with entire family units rather than the individual	Other	2.70 (0.90)	20
16. Assisting clients to identify their expectations about substance use	CB	3.48 (0.64)	55
17. Using Native American spirituality concepts	Other	1.93 (0.88)	5
18. Identifying client attributions–whether they blame themselves or others for bad things that happen to them	CB	3.42 (0.67)	51
19. Assisting clients to take a personal inventory of their lives	AA	3.37 (0.76)	52
20. Recognizing that the style and warmth of the counselor is a powerful factor in treatment	ME	3.83 (0.44)	85
21. Helping clients link behavior to rewards and punishments in their environment	Beh	3.57 (0.58)	61
22. Using culturally-specific activities when appropriate	CC	3.20 (0.86)	35

TABLE 5 (continued)

Principle/technique	Fidelity Scale	Mean (SD)	% who use it often
23. Creating discrepancies to help clients understand their behavior	ME	3.23 (0.78)	43
24. Providing opportunities for clients to practice new behaviors in real-life contexts	Beh	3.23 (0.78)	41
25. Using techniques such as push-ups, pulls-ups, and learning experiences	TC	2.05 (1.01)	10
26. Role-playing to practice new skills	CB	2.86 (0.88)	23
27. Helping clients realize that they can change the way they think about alcohol and drug use	CB	3.86 (0.37)	87
28. Reflecting back things that clients say	ME	3.81 (0.42)	82
29. Avoiding imposing values on clients	CC	3.73 (0.60)	80
30. Helping clients recognize the power of unconscious thoughts	Freud	3.00 (0.91)	35
31. Recognizing the value of and using ambivalence of clients to motivate them	ME	3.20 (0.77)	38
32. Helping family members see when they are enabling the substance abuser	Other	3.01 (0.97)	38
33. Giving clients concrete rewards for positive behavior	Beh	2.75 (1.00)	27
34. Knowing when to "roll" with their resistance	ME	3.51 (0.61)	56
35. Providing anger management activities	Other	3.44 (0.70)	54
36. Finding mentors or sponsors for my clients	12	2.36 (1.04)	18
37. Developing a strong peer support environment in my treatment center	TC	3.36 (0.85)	56
38. Giving clients responsibility for self-governance within the unit or group	TC	3.26 (0.84)	47
39. Displaying genuineness and unconditional positive regard for clients	CC	3.93 (0.26)	93
40. Addressing the clients physical health, fitness and nutrition needs	CC	3.57 (0.62)	63
41. Helping clients discover their higher power	12	3.06 (0.81)	32
42. Fostering exploration of early childhood experiences	Freud	2.69 (0.92)	22
43. Avoiding confrontation and breaking down denial or defense mechanisms until a strong working alliance has been built with the client	ME	3.42 (0.77)	56

Principle/technique	Fidelity Scale	Mean (SD)	% who use it often
44. Assisting clients in separating their worth/value from their actions	CB	3.63 (0.60)	68
45. Using self-appraisal skills–helping clients to see how they perceive their own behavior	CB	3.55 (0.58)	59
46. Supporting development of self-efficacy	ME	3.67 (0.50)	69
47. Establishing healthy boundaries and ground rules	CC	3.84 (0.39)	85
48. Breaking co-dependency patterns in family members	Other	2.89 (0.95)	30
49. Role modeling healthy lifestyles and/or skills	CC	3.71 (0.53)	74
50. Using affirmations–positive feedback	ME	3.88 (0.37)	90
51. Expressing empathy for a client	CC	3.89 (0.33)	89

Key: 1 = never; 2 = rarely; 3 = sometimes; 4 = often
Models: 12 = 12 step; ME = Motivational Enhancement; Freud = Freudian/psychodynamic; CB = Cognitive Behavioral; Beh = Behavioral; TC = Therapeutic Community; CC = Basic counselor competency; Other = other specific techniques/principles not associated with a model.

on the fidelity scales were widely used practices that might apply to several treatment approaches, but only two of the most often endorsed items were associated with a specific treatment model (both related to cognitions). The most commonly endorsed items were:

- Display genuineness and positive regard for clients (93%)
- Educate clients on signs and symptoms of relapse and help them identify triggers (91%)
- Express empathy for clients (89%)
- Help clients recognize they can change the way they think about alcohol and drug use (87%)
- Help clients to recognize faulty thinking patterns (86%)
- Establish healthy boundaries and ground rules (85%)

Table 6 shows the relationships among the treatment models in terms of what percent of respondents were trained in them, which ones counselors reported that they felt competent to use, what approach characterized their usual practice, and what approach characterized their agencies as a whole. Reporting training and feeling competent to use the approach were congruent for 12 step, cognitive-behavioral and motivational enhancement approaches. On the other hand, counselors were less likely to report congruence between training and perceived compe-

TABLE 6. The relationship between training, perceived competency, and use of approaches

Approach	Trained in (%)	Competent in (%)	Usual practice (%)	Agency practice (%)
12 step	60	66	47	49
Cognitive behavioral	91	92	81	73
Motivational enhancement	75	65	51	45
Matrix model	27	13	4	11
Behavioral	43	26	10	8
Therapeutic community	54	40	24	21
Psychodynamic	56	19	8	3

tency for the other approaches. The most striking difference was between psychodynamic training (56%) and perceived competency (19%).

The Impact of Recovery on Counselor Practices and Treatment Philosophies

We compared counselors who reported that they were in recovery from substance abuse (n = 71) to those who were not (n = 126). When asked what approach they used in their daily practice, counselors in recovery were much more likely to report use of a 12 step model (70%) than counselors not in recovery (34%; Chi square = 24.0, df = 1, p < .0001). Counselors in recovery were also somewhat less likely to report using a cognitive behavioral approach than counselors not in recovery, although the difference is much smaller (73% of those in recovery and 86% of those not in recovery reported use of cognitive behavioral methods, Chi square = 4.6, df = 1, p < 0.03). Although there was at least one significant difference in the type of model used (i.e., counselors in recovery were much more likely to report the use of a 12 step approach), there were statistically significant differences on only 4 of the 51 items on the fidelity scales. Counselors in recovery were more likely to report that they educated clients on the disease model of addiction (mean of 3.4 for counselors not in recovery and 3.7 for those in recovery), use Native American spirituality concepts (mean of 1.7 for those not in recovery and 2.3 for those in recovery), use culturally-specific activities (mean of 3.0 for those not in recovery and 3.3 for those in recovery), and help clients recognize the power of unconscious thoughts (mean of 2.9 for those not in recovery and 3.2 for those in recovery). All of these differences were significant at the $p < .01$ level. We also included an open-ended item about the impact that recovery had on their practice. The most common responses are listed below:

- Being in recovery gives me greater understanding and insight into the addiction process (22 responses)
- Being in recovery gives me more empathy for the client and/or allows clients to relate to me easier (21 responses)
- Being in recovery is the motivation for doing this work (8 responses)
- My own practice with substance abuse clients helps me to keep clean and sober (constant working with the steps or with the recovery process) (5 responses)

What Materials Counselors Used to Improve Their Practice

Respondents in this study reported spending about 3 hours per week updating their skills and preparing to work with clients. We included an open-ended question about the resources that counselors find helpful to them in their practice. As expected, there was a wide variation in responding, but we categorized them into groups as follows:

- Self-help books (50)
- 12 step materials such as Big Book, pamphlets, workbooks (47)
- CSAT TIPS and TAPS (36)
- Professional/academic books (27)
- Specific manuals or curriculum materials (22)
- The Diagnostic and Statistical Manual (DSM) (19)
- Cognitive Behavioral materials, unspecified (18)
- Handouts, worksheets from workshops (14)
- Motivational Enhancement materials, unspecified (10)
- Internet resources (7)
- ASAM criteria (6)
- Professional journals (6)

DISCUSSION

The study has a number of limitations that may impact the findings. First, nearly half of the respondents were drawn from a conference, where one might expect counselors who are more highly motivated to learn. Secondly, they are highly educated with many respondents having master's degrees in counseling fields, 37% of them with formal education in substance abuse counseling. However, if any group of counselor would be likely to apply research findings to practice or report that they engaged in theory-guided practice, this highly educated group would be ideally suited. The instrument assessed self-report information about treatment orientations and techniques, and we have no way of validating that the respondents actually use these techniques in practice. It may be that counselors have endorsed use of one approach, but over time, they have converted the techniques or language of that approach into everyday language, altering the original approach. That is, a counselor may attend training on cognitive behavioral skills training and upon applying it in their own work, translate the language to be more appropriate to the client base. This translation may or may not preserve the original intent of the approach. The counselor may still believe that he/she is using a cognitive behavioral approach, but the specific techniques may be different from the training skills.

The main findings of the study were that substance abuse treatment counselors reported using multiple and sometimes contradictory theoretical models to guide their practice, and that their actual daily work is characterized more by eclectic combinations of techniques than by theory-driven practice. This supports other research on counselor treatment orientations.[4,11] There are at least three ways to interpret the finding that substance abuse counselors do not appear to practice the approaches they say they use in their daily work. First, it may be that counselors do not use theoretical frameworks or models to guide their practice, but instead truly do use eclectic collections of techniques or practices that suit their own style of counseling or reflect the most recent workshop training or class that they have experienced. Another possibility is that the major theoretical frameworks for the models we chose overlap to a great extent, so the analyses of fidelity scales are not clear cut because the concepts are too interrelated. Finally, counselors may translate theory or research concepts into everyday language, examples, or skills that may or may not preserve the integrity of the original training. It is difficult to evaluate whether they are still using an evidence-based practice. Most likely the answer is a combination of all of these—the treatment approaches do overlap to a great extent and substance abuse counselors, like other counseling professionals, gravitate to eclectic practices that suit their client needs and own individual styles and/or translate research or theoretical concepts into language they and clients can readily understand or relate to.

Implications for the Field

Researchers embarking on experimental research testing treatment effectiveness need to take into account that there is no typical or usual substance abuse treatment practice. However, having knowledge of the procedures that counselors are actually using prior to training on some new approach can be used as a pre-test or a baseline. Theoretically, good training should help the trainee to identify the cluster of activities that accompany the approach and strengthen their use while at the same time decreasing use of techniques that are in opposition to the trained approach. For example, counselors who use confrontational methods should decrease the use of these techniques after training in motivational enhancement.

The finding that counselors often use techniques that are in opposition to the theoretical approaches that they say characterize their practice may be related to a lack of basic understanding of the theoretical frameworks that underlie the most common counseling approaches. It is possible that training may have focused on specific techniques or applications without the theoretical background. Thus, to professionalize the field and put counseling approaches into perspective, training should include some discussion of the theoretical framework and how the approach differs philosophically from other approaches.

Treatment counselors use a wide variety of materials to enhance their practice, but only rarely use academic or professional materials. There is a great need to translate research into practice in forms that counselors will use. Some of the handouts they collect at conferences and workshops may reflect research to practice methods, but we cannot tell from our data. The reliance on self-help books is not surprising–these lay out information in a simple manner and often offer concrete activities, worksheets, and/or assignments to address common treatment issues such as self-esteem, anger, "addictive thinking," and other concepts. Even though 12 step approaches were reported by less than half of the sample, 12 step materials were the second most common type of resource used for daily practice. Fortunately, CSAT's TIPS and TAPS were widely used and many counselors referred to them by name or number, such as the TIP on stimulant abuse. However, respondents in this sample only rarely consulted professional journals or used the internet to access resources. This data highlight the need for materials that translate research into practice in order to decrease the reliance on lay press materials.

Counselors in recovery reported that they use a 12 step treatment philosophy more often than counselors not in recovery, but they did not differ on their actual daily practices. Recovery status was seen as a tool to relate better to clients, have clients develop rapport more quickly, and as a motivator to stay in a field with high burnout and turnover. However, in actual daily practice, there seemed to be very little difference among those in recovery and those counselors who were not in recovery themselves.

One rather disheartening finding was that majority of counselors (64%) believed that their clients were not motivated to change, and the vast majority (76%) felt that most of their clients would never achieve long-term sobriety. If counselors do not believe that clients will recover, are these attitudes conveyed in subtle manner to their clients? Kasarabada et al.[15] found that counselor attributes such as nurturance, openness, and genuineness were positively related to client outcomes. There is a common belief that recovering addicts are adept at identifying "phonies" thus may perceive a counselor's lack of belief in their ability to recover. The stigma of substance abuse appears to affect not only people in the general population, but also substance abuse treatment counselors.

In conclusion, the main results of this study suggested that there may be no such thing as "treatment as usual" but instead, many highly individual and eclectic combinations of techniques and principles. Some of these eclectic techniques are compatible with an evidence-based practice, but we know very little about hybrid approaches. Motivational enhancement and 12 step approaches may both have empirical evidence to support their use, but what about a blend of some ME techniques and some 12 step techniques? Both the current study and work by Ogborne and colleagues[11] found a psychodynamic-behavioral hybrid approach, warranting further study. It appears that there is a great need to develop training and technology transfer strategies that help counselors achieve a consistent approach to treatment, using models that have been shown to be effective. However, there may also be value in studying the effectiveness of hybrid approaches since they are so common in the field.

REFERENCES

1. Lamb S, Greenlick MR, McCarty D. Bridging the gap between practice and research: forging partnerships with community-based drug and alcohol treatment. 1998; Washington, DC: National Academy Press.

2. Project Match Research Group. Matching alcoholism treatments to client heterogeneity: Project MATCH Posttreatment drinking outcomes. Journal of Studies on Alcohol. 1997; 58(1):7-29.

3. Allen K. Attitudes of registered nurses toward alcoholic patients in a general hospital population. International Journal of the Addictions. 1993; 2:923-930.

4. Ball S, Bachrach K, DeCarlo J, Farentinos C, Keen M, McSherry TL, Polcin D, Snead N, Sockriter R, Wrigley P, Zammarelli L, Carroll K. Characteristics, beliefs, and practices of community clinicians trained to provide manual-guided therapy for substance abusers. Journal of Substance Abuse Treatment. 2002; 23(4): 309-318.

5. Capelhorn JR, Hartel DM, Irwig L. Measuring the attitudes and beliefs of staff working in New York methadone maintenance clinics. Substance Use and Misuse. 1997; 21:299-413.

6. Humphreys K, Noke JM, Moos RH. Recovering substance abuse staff members' beliefs about addiction. Journal of Substance Abuse Treatment. 1995; 13:75-78.

7. McDowell D, Galanter M, Goldfarb L, Lifschutz H. Spirituality and the treatment of the dually diagnosed: an investigation of patient and staff attitudes. Journal of Addictive Diseases. 1996; 15:55-68.

8. Carrol J. Attitudes to drug users according to age of staff. Professional Nurse. 1996; 11:401-404.

9. Ogborne AC, Braun, K, Schmidt G. Working in addictions treatment services: some views of a sample of service providers in Ontario. Substance Use and Misuse. 1998; 33:2425-2440.

10. Forman RF, Bovasso G, Woody G. Staff beliefs about addiction treatment. Journal of Substance Abuse Treatment. 2001; 21:1-9.

11. Ogborne A, Wild C, Braun K, Newton-Taylor B. Measuring treatment process beliefs among staff of specialized addiction treatment services. Journal of Substance Abuse Treatment. 1998; 15:301-312.

12. Center for Substance Abuse Treatment. Addiction Counseling Competencies: The knowledge, skills, and attitudes of professional practice, 1998. Rockville, MD: USDHHS, SAMHSA, TAP #21.

13. Arndt S. Multiple group factor analysis. American Statistician. 1983; 37:326.

14. Gorsuch RL. Factor analysis. 1974. Philadelphia, PA: W.B. Saunders Co.

15. Kasarabada N, Hser Y, Boles S, Huang Y. Do patients' perceptions of their counselors influence outcomes of drug treatment? Journal of Substance Abuse Treatment. 2002; 23:327-334.

Use of Opinion Leaders
and Intensive Training
to Implement Evidence-Based
Co-Occurring Disorders Treatment
in the Community

Roger H. Peters, PhD
Kathleen A. Moore, PhD
Holly A. Hills, PhD
M. Scott Young, PhD
James B. LeVasseur, PhD
Alexander R. Rich, PhD
W. Michael Hunt, PhD
Thomas W. Valente, PhD

Roger H. Peters, Kathleen A. Moore, Holly A. Hills, M. Scott Young, James B. LeVasseur, Alexander R. Rich, and W. Michael Hunt are affiliated with the Department of Mental Health Law and Policy, Louis de la Parte Florida Mental Health Institute, University of South Florida.

Thomas W. Valente is affiliated with the Department of Preventive Medicine, University of Southern California.

Address correspondence to: Roger H. Peters, PhD, Department of Mental Health Law and Policy, Florida Mental Health Institute, University of South Florida, 13301 Bruce B. Downs Boulevard, Tampa, FL 33612 (E-mail: peters@fmhi.usf.edu).

[Haworth co-indexing entry note]: "Use of Opinion Leaders and Intensive Training to Implement Evidence-Based Co-Occurring Disorders Treatment in the Community." Peters, Roger H. et al. Co-published simultaneously in *Journal of Addictive Diseases* (The Haworth Medical Press, an imprint of The Haworth Press, Inc.) Vol. 24, Supplement No. 1, 2005, pp. 53-74; and: *Implementing Evidence-Based Practices for Treatment of Alcohol and Drug Disorders* (ed: Eldon Edmundson, Jr., and Dennis McCarty) The Haworth Medical Press, an imprint of The Haworth Press, Inc., 2005, pp. 53-74. Single or multiple copies of this article are available for a fee from The Haworth Document Delivery Service [1-800-HAWORTH, 9:00 a.m. - 5:00 p.m. (EST). E-mail address: docdelivery@haworthpress.com].

SUMMARY. Although several evidence-based substance abuse treatment interventions have been developed in recent years, efforts to translate this new knowledge to practice settings have been largely discouraging.[1,2] The current study examines results from a SAMHSA/CSAT-funded Practice Improvement Collaborative project in Tampa, Florida, developed to facilitate the implementation of an evidence-based manualized treatment approach for clients with co-occurring mental health and substance use disorders. A quasi-experimental design was used to examine the effectiveness of intensive counselor training sessions and use of peer opinion leaders to monitor and supervise counselor's implementation of the manualized treatment approach, in comparison to a standard training session and resource materials provided to counselors.

A total of 43 counselors in the experimental group and 28 counselors in the comparison group completed baseline and three-month follow-up measures to examine the extent of manual implementation, and changes in treatment practices, attitudes, knowledge acquisition, and work-related behaviors related to co-occurring disorders treatment. Findings indicate a significantly higher rate of manual implementation among counselors who received a structured series of opinion leader-facilitated training and consultative activities, in comparison to counselors who received only a traditional training workshop. The experimental group also indicated significantly greater use of evidence-based practices in their work from the baseline to follow-up period, relative to comparison group counselors, although group differences were not detected in attitudinal change or knowledge acquisition. Results provide evidence for the effectiveness of enhanced training regimens that are coupled with use of peer opinion leaders in implementing evidence-based practices in community substance abuse treatment settings. *[Article copies available for a fee from The Haworth Document Delivery Service: 1-800-HAWORTH. E-mail address: <docdelivery@haworthpress.com> Website: <http://www.HaworthPress.com> © 2005 by The Haworth Press, Inc. All rights reserved.]*

KEYWORDS. Substance abuse, co-occurring disorders, technology transfer, opinion leader, manualized treatment

INTRODUCTION

The empirical base for effective substance abuse treatment has rapidly developed over the past two decades.[3,4] It is increasingly apparent, however, that many of these advances have not been quickly adapted into clinical practice.[5,6] Several factors contribute to this delay in technology transfer, including: (1) limited communication and collaboration between service providers and researchers, (2) lack of awareness of emerging treatment approaches, (3) concerns regarding feasibility or cost of interventions, (4) limited generalizability of new treatment approaches in clinical settings, and (5) lack of resources for training and technical assistance.[1,5,7,8]

A range of organizational factors (e.g., readiness for change) and staff characteristics also influence the adoption of new treatment practices.[9-11] For example, service providers are often unaware of effective technology transfer approaches, and have not traditionally developed organizational strategies to implement new treatment practices. Without agency-level endorsement and a comprehensive implementation plan, the transfer of practice innovations to treatment settings has been poorly received by both staff and clients.[1,2] Failure to accomplish technology transfer in the substance abuse treatment arena is thought to account for poor client retention rates, high rates of substance use relapse and criminal recidivism, and low morale and high turnover among line staff.[12]

Increased attention has recently focused on technology transfer approaches in health services settings that involve interpersonal contact with line staff, and involvement of clinicians and administrators in the adoption process.[13] These approaches are based on findings that individual instruction and feedback, and negotiation among staff in developing and implementing new interventions has a considerable impact on the adoption process.[14] Various strategies have been documented for providing academic detailing, outreach, and sequential training or consultation activities to influence peers' implementation of new interventions.[15,16] These interpersonal technology transfer strategies are generally enhanced through use of credible organizational champions or peer opinion leaders, who often serve as central sources of information and an impetus for innovation and change.[17-19] These opinion leaders can be readily identified through use of a network analysis conducted within a particular organization.[18-22]

Opinion leaders can be instrumental in establishing the credibility of health care interventions and for facilitating their diffusion and implementation.[19,23,24] Opinion leaders have been shown to effectively facilitate the transfer of new information in substance abuse treatment and other health-related settings.[17,19,21,23-25] Examples of opinion leaders that have been successfully employed in health-related technology transfer applications include the training of gay men to endorse safe sexual practices to their peers,[23] and the use of peer physicians to encourage adherence to best practice guidelines related to medical management of women with a history of cesarean section,[24] and to improve the quality of care among patients with acute myocardial infarction (AMI).[26] Within the substance abuse field, opinion leaders have successfully facilitated the adoption and implementation of evidence-based prevention practices,[27-30] including interventions found to be effective in preventing smoking and substance abuse among adolescents and young adults.

The current study examined the effectiveness of peer opinion leaders in providing a structured series of training and consultative activities with counselors in community-based substance abuse agencies, to assist them in implementing an evidence-based, manualized treatment curriculum. The purpose of the study was not to examine client outcomes related to implementation of the evidenced-based treatment. Instead, patterns of implementation of the manualized treatment were compared for counselors who were provided the structured opinion leader training and consultation, and for counselors who received copies of the manual and a general training workshop, with no opinion leader involvement.

An initial pilot study conducted by project staff led to the identification, adaptation, and field-testing of an evidence-based manualized treatment curriculum designed for clients who have co-occurring mental health and substance abuse disorders. The treatment manual was adapted from materials developed by the New Hampshire-Dartmouth Psychiatric Research Center.[31] This topic area was selected based on results of a needs assessment conducted with community treatment agencies in the Tampa Bay area.[32] Based on recent evidence of the influential nature of opinion leaders in facilitating technology transfer in health-related settings,[23-25] the current study examined the impact of opinion leaders in assisting peer counselors to implement the co-occurring disorders treatment manual (hereafter described as the "treatment manual") during a three-month operational period. The main hypothesis of the study was that counselors who received a structured series of training and consultation provided by peer opinion leaders would be more likely to use the manual in group treatment sessions during the three-month implementation period, in comparison to counselors who received only a general training and no exposure to opinion leaders. Secondary hypotheses were that counselors in the experimental condition would experience greater improvements in knowledge acquisition, attitudes, and practice behaviors related to co-occurring disorders, in contrast to counselors in the comparison sample.

METHOD

Participants

Four community-based agencies were selected to participate in the study. These included the three largest publicly funded substance abuse treatment agencies (ACTS, Inc., DACCO, Inc., Operation PAR, Inc.) in the Tampa Bay area and a jail-based treatment program (Hillsborough County Sheriff's Office). Each of the publicly funded treatment agencies provides a full range of outpatient, residential, and other services. In order to provide diversity in implementation sites, 10 programs were selected from these four agencies. Both outpatient and residential programs were included that served clients who have co-occurring disorders. Counselors selected from these programs were those who had primary work assignments related to direct client contact and other support activities. A total of 43 counselors from the 10 treatment programs were selected for inclusion in the study.

The Center for Drug Free Living in Orlando, Florida was selected as the comparison site for the study. The Center for Drug Free Living is the largest publicly funded substance abuse treatment provider in Orlando, and provides a full array of outpatient and residential services that are comparable to those provided in the Tampa treatment sites. The Center for Drug Free Living serves a wide range of clients who have substance abuse and co-occurring disorders, and has successfully participated in a number of federally funded research projects, including the NIDA Clinical Trials Network. The comparison site is also geographically separate (90 miles in distance) from the Tampa Bay area, providing an opportunity to minimize diffusion of the experimental procedure that was implemented in the participating Tampa Bay agencies. A total of 28 counselors were recruited from seven treatment programs within the comparison site. These counselors were identified as those who volunteered to participate in the current study, and who worked with clients with co-occurring disorders.

Development of a Manualized Treatment Protocol

A community needs assessment was implemented as part of the project. The needs assessment helped to prioritize the area of co-occurring disorders treatment as the focus for the manualized treatment to be implemented in the study. An extensive literature review was then conducted, and an expert panel convened for the purpose of identifying an evidence-based co-occurring disorders treatment manual for use in the study. The panel included several national experts in the co-occurring disorders area, in addition to administrators, counselors, and clients from the participating treatment agencies in the Tampa Bay area.

Based on the literature review and recommendations of the expert panel, a treatment manual was selected for use in the study that was developed by the New Hampshire-Dartmouth Psychiatric Research Center.[31] The treatment manual was adapted for the current study through consultation with the expert panel, faculty at the New Hampshire-Dartmouth Psychiatric Research Center, and representatives from each of the participating treatment agencies in the Tampa Bay area. The treatment manual adapted for the current study included eight psycho-educational modules,[33] and was intended for administration in a group treatment setting. Each of the group treatment modules required approximately 60 to 90 minutes to administer. Each module addressed a separate theme (e.g., substance use and depressive disorders) and described the interactive nature of the particular disorders, medications used to treat co-occurring disorders, and key treatment strategies. In addition to addressing the interactive effects of major mental health disorders and co-occurring substance use disorders, the manual examined relapse prevention approaches and risk factors for co-occurring disorders, and provided an inventory of specialized co-occurring disorders services that were indicated for program participants. The treatment manual was field tested and revised through consultation with clients and staff from each of the participating treatment agencies, and a companion workbook was created for clients.

Selection of Opinion Leaders

Network analysis techniques[21] were used to identify an opinion leader from each of the 10 participating treatment programs in the experimental group. In order to identify opinion leaders, all counselors were surveyed and asked to respond to the following question: "From among your co-workers, whom would you go to if you had questions about a client who might have co-occurring mental health and substance abuse problems?" The question was intended to identify individuals who were perceived by their coworkers as having the most expertise related to co-occurring disorders treatment, and who therefore were the most sought after by agency counselors for such information. Ten opinion leaders were identified through this process, including three each from ACTS, DACCO, and PAR, and one from the Hillsborough County

Sheriff's Office. The opinion leaders were then recruited to participate in the study, and were paid $500 for their involvement in training, consultation, and data collection activities.

Training and Consultation Related to the Treatment Manual

Training related to counselor's use of the treatment manual took place in three different phases. The first phase (Foundations training) was offered to counselors in both the experimental and comparison groups, while the second (Opinion Leader training) and third (Counselor training) phases were provided only to counselors in the experimental group. The 4-hour Foundations training was provided to all counselors participating in the experimental and comparison groups, and was presented by several of the project staff as a continuing education workshop. The Foundations training focused on general principles of assessment and treatment of co-occurring disorders, rather than on the treatment manual. This training included a review of integrated treatment approaches that have been found to be effective for clients with co-occurring disorders.

The Opinion Leader training was provided only to designated opinion leaders from the 10 treatment programs, who participated in a two-day training workshop that addressed use of the treatment manual and methods to facilitate counselor engagement in the manual's implementation. This training was provided by a faculty member at the New Hampshire-Dartmouth Psychiatric Research Center who is an expert in the co-occurring disorders treatment area, and consisted of didactic instruction, role-play sessions using questions and exercises contained in the manual, and review of other materials from the treatment manual. The third phase of training (Counselor training) was provided by the 10 opinion leaders for counselors working within their own treatment programs. The Counselor training consisted of a 90-minute session that reviewed the psychoeducational modules, demonstrated how to implement the treatment manual in group treatment sessions, and provided clinical strategies for engaging clients in the treatment groups. Following implementation of the treatment manual, opinion leaders in each of the 10 participating programs met weekly with treatment counselors in their program to provide ongoing consultation regarding implementation of the treatment manual, and to address questions and concerns about the manual.

Implementation of the Treatment Manual

Once opinion leaders received training, and trained their program's counselors in use of the treatment manual, counselors in each of the 10 treatment programs were asked to introduce the manual in group treatment sessions during a three-month implementation period. Each treatment counselor in the experimental group received a copy of the manual, and copies of a companion workbook were distributed to clients. Each treatment counselor in the comparison group was also mailed a copy of the treatment manual and a copy of the client workbook, along with a letter describing the manual as an evidence-based treatment protocol for use with clients who have co-occurring disorders.

Opinion leaders submitted weekly progress reports to project staff to verify implementation of the manual and to identify any concerns related to this process. These reports documented the sequence in which modules were presented, and the response to each module by both counselors and clients. Project staff observed one randomly selected treatment session for each of the 10 participating treatment programs, in order to assess fidelity in administration of the treatment manual. No additional study-related opinion leader training or consultation activities were provided following completion of the three-month implementation period, nor did the opinion leaders receive additional payments from the study after this time.

Measures

Demographic and background history measures. Each counselor participating in the study completed a brief questionnaire that provided demographic information and described their educational and vocational experience.

Organizational readiness for change. The Texas Christian University Organizational Readiness for Change instrument (ORC)[34] was administered to counselors in the experimental and comparison groups to examine organizational factors that might influence technology transfer. The ORC measure was developed to examine organizational readiness for change, resources, cohesion, stress, and patterns of communication, and has been found to have satisfactory psychometric properties.

Counselor adoption of the treatment manual. A follow-up counselor self-report instrument was developed to obtain information regarding counselor's past and current use of the treatment manual and to assess the level of adoption of these materials. Counselors were also asked if they intended to use the treatment manual in the future, and whether they intended to use "none," "some," or "all" of the treatment manual materials in the future. Finally, the self-report instrument assessed the extent to which counselors believed that the treatment manual added important clinical information for their program.

Counselor time allocation. A self-report instrument included questions to assess the number of hours each week that counselors spent working with clients who have co-occurring disorders, and the number of hours each week spent discussing (with coworkers and supervisors) issues related to clients who have co-occurring disorders. Counselors were also asked to indicate the approximate number of minutes spent each week discussing issues related to co-occurring disorders in their treatment groups.

Counselor attitudes and practices related to co-occurring disorders. A review of the literature yielded no salient measures that had been previously developed to assess counselor practice behaviors and attitudes related to clients who have co-occurring disorders. As a result, two scales were developed by project research staff for use in the current study. The Co-Occurring Disorders Treatment-Practice Scale (CDTPS) was designed to assess counselors' current clinical practices related to co-occurring disorders, with a particular focus on the use of evidence-based approaches. The Co-Occurring Disorders Treatment-Attitudes Scale (CDTAS) was designed to assess counselors' attitudes towards clients who have co-occurring disorders. Each scale elicits counselor ratings on a five-point Likert scale (1 = "strongly disagree," 5 = "strongly agree"). Some items on the CDTPS and CDTAS were reverse coded to insure that higher scores on items uniformly reflected more desirable attitudes and practices.

The CDTPS includes 15 items and has an internal consistency (alpha) of .80. The CDTPS consists of items describing referral for co-occurring disorders treatment services, evidence-based co-occurring disorders treatment practices, and assessment of co-occurring disorders. Referral items on the CDTPS describe whether clients are routed to appropriate services for their co-occurring disorders (e.g., "I always know where to go to get medication for clients with mental illness"). Evidence-based practice items examine the extent to which counselors use evidenced-based clinical interventions in their work (e.g., " We use structured interventions such as specialized manuals and exercises for treating clients with co-occurring mental illness and substance abuse problems"). Assessment items investigate whether counselors use appropriate assessments approaches with clients who have co-occurring disorders (e.g., "When a client is identified as having a co-occurring mental illness and substance abuse problem this information does not change the nature of the treatment plan with us").

The CDTAS includes 12 items and has an internal consistency of .72. The CDTAS examines various different types of attitudes towards clients who have co-occurring disorders and about their response to treatment, and includes items that address counselor confidence in their ability to work with clients who have co-occurring disorders (e.g., "It is difficult for me to know when a client may need an evaluation for medication for mental illness"). The CDTAS also describes counselors' willingness to work with clients who have co-occurring disorders (e.g., "Clients with both substance abuse and mental illness problems should not be served in this program"), and counselors' perceived prognosis for treatment among clients with co-occurring disorders (e.g., "For the most part, it is a hopeless cause trying to help someone with both mental illness and substance abuse problems").

Counselor knowledge related to co-occurring disorders. A review of the literature yielded no previously developed measures to assess counselor knowledge related to co-occurring disorders. As a result, the Co-Occurring Disorders Knowledge Test (CODKT) was specifically designed for this study to measure counselor knowledge in this area. Project research staff generated 19 items examining co-occurring disorders and related evidence-based treatment approaches. The CODKT instrument addressed risk factors related to major mental health and substance use disorders, symptoms of these disorders, interactive effects of the two types of disorders, and treatment approaches for these disorders. The CODKT, which had an internal consistency of .69 uses a multiple-choice format with five potential responses to each question. The highest possible score on the instrument is 38, with zero, one, or two points awarded for incorrect, partially correct, or the best possible answer, respectively. The CODKT was not specifically keyed to information furnished in the Foundations training or in the treatment manual.

Experimental Procedure and Design

A baseline counselor self-report instrument was completed by all participants at the onset of the Foundations training. The baseline instrument included the CDTPS, the CDTAS, the CODKT, a time allocation measure, and the demographic and background history questionnaire. Following completion of the structured series of training workshops (Foundations training, Opinion Leader training, and Counselor training), counselors were instructed to implement the treatment manual in their treatment groups. Opinion leaders held weekly consultation sessions with counselors within their own treatment program. Three months was allowed for complete implementation of the 8-module treatment manual in each of the 10 program sites.

Within one month following the conclusion of the implementation period, all counselors in both the experimental and comparison groups were contacted and completed a post-implementation follow-up counselor self-report instrument. This follow-up instrument included questions to assess counselors' implementation of the treatment manual, and their opinions regarding the quality and usefulness of the manual. The follow-up instrument also included the time allocation items from the baseline counselor self-report, the CDTPS and CDTAS scales, and the CODKT. Counselors in the experimental group were contacted again within six months following the conclusion of the implementation period, and completed a six-month follow-up self-report instrument that included the same elements as the post-implementation follow-up instrument.

The current study used a quasi-experimental, pre-post implementation research design with nonrandom assignment of counselors to the two conditions. Chi-square analyses were used to examine between-groups differences on the categorical variables probing counselors' adoption of, and reaction to the manualized curriculum. Changes from baseline to post-implementation related to time allocation, the CDTPS and CDTAS scales, and the CODKT were examined for between-groups differences using analyses of covariance (ANCOVAs). Gender, age, and educational level were entered as covariates to control for their variance at baseline (see Table 1). Baseline scores were also covaried, and post-implementation scores served as dependent measures to examine change over time. Group assignment (experimental or comparison group) was used as the between-groups factor. Within subjects repeated measures analyses of variance were used to test whether changes in experimental group counselor attitudes, practices, and knowledge from baseline to post-implementation were maintained during an extended follow-up period.

RESULTS

Characteristics of Experimental and Comparison Samples

Table 1 describes demographic and vocational characteristics of the experimental and comparison groups. The comparison group had a sig-

TABLE 1. Demographic, background, and vocational information by group

	Experimental Group (n = 43)	Comparison Group (n = 28)	Significance
Gender: Females	63%	86%	χ^2 (1, N = 71) = 4.40*
Race/Ethnicity:			
Caucasian	67%	67%	
African-American	25%	15%	χ^2 (3, N = 67) = 2.96
Asian/Pacific Islander	3%	11%	
Hispanic	5%	7%	
Age	47.43 (11.66)	40.93 (10.95)	t(65) = 2.29*
Education:			
At least master's degree	34%	75%	χ^2 (1, N = 69) = 11.10**
At least one certification	35%	43%	χ^2 (1, N = 71) = 0.46
# formal courses in SA	12.78 (14.11)	8.64 (13.80)	t(58) = 1.13
# formal courses in MH	8.88 (11.21)	7.24 (11.13)	t(55) = 0.55
Years Experience:			
Co-occurring disorders treatment	6.63 (5.37)	6.10 (7.51)	t(65) = 0.33
Substance abuse treatment	7.02 (5.54)	4.68 (5.37)	t(66) = −1.73
Mental health treatment	5.97 (6.52)	6.83 (8.26)	t(63) = −0.47
Adult services	11.65 (9.71)	7.69 (7.07)	t(65) = −1.82
Training:			
# past year SA training hours	21.82 (22.40)	13.15 (19.43)	t(63) = 1.62
# past year MH training hours	11.44 (18.37)	7.80 (12.46)	t(58) = −0.86
# past year co-occurring disorders training hours	9.59 (16.91)	3.63 (5.17)	t(57) = −1.67
Years employed in current program	4.84 (4.66)	2.88 (3.90)	t(66) = −1.80

Note. Means are followed by standard deviations in parentheses.
* $p < .05$.
** $p < .01$.

nificantly higher proportion of female counselors, and was significantly younger by an average of approximately six years (41 versus 47). Additionally, a significantly higher proportion of counselors from the comparison group had at least a master's degree (75% versus 34%). No other significant differences were noted with respect to educational background or experience in substance abuse or mental health treatment. However, counselors in the experimental group had slightly but not significantly more training in the past year related to substance abuse, mental health, and co-occurring disorders treatment. Counselors from the comparison group reported significantly better physical resources in the workplace (e.g., office space, computer access) relative to the experimental group, as measured by the Texas Christian University

Organizational Readiness for Change instrument. Counselors in the comparison group also reported better cohesion and communication, organization, and less organizational stress, relative to counselors in the experimental group. The groups did not differ in measures of organizational motivation for change.

Implementation of the Evidence-Based Treatment Manual

Table 2 describes results related to counselors' implementation of the evidence-based treatment manual. Each of the counselors who were exposed to opinion leaders and the structured training and consultation regimen reported that they implemented the treatment manual during the three-month study period. In contrast, significantly fewer (19%) counselors from the comparison group reported implementation of the treatment manual, χ^2 (1, N = 69) = 49.93, p < .001. Consistent with these results, a significantly greater proportion of counselors in the experimental group reported that they currently use the manual (48% vs. 19%), χ^2 (1, N = 68) = 5.67, p < .05, or planned to use the manual in the future (95% versus 52%), χ^2 (1, N = 67) = 17.73, p < .001, relative to the comparison group. As indicated in Table 2, significantly more counselors in the experimental group (93%) than the comparison group (48%) reported that the manual provided important clinical information about co-occurring disorders, χ^2 (1, N = 64) = 16.52, p < .001.

TABLE 2. Use of the evidence-based co-occurring disorders treatment manual by group

	Post-Implementation		Post-Implementation Between Groups Significance Test	6-Month Follow-Up
	Experimental Group (%) (n = 43)	Comparison Group (%) (n = 28)		Experimental Group (%) (n = 39)
Past 6 Month manual use	100	19	χ^2 (1, N = 69) = 49.93***	81
Current manual use	48	19	χ^2 (1, N = 68) = 5.67*	52
Plan to use manual in the Future	95	52	χ^2 (1, N = 67) = 17.73***	97
Manual adds important clinical information	93	48	χ^2 (1, N = 64) = 16.52***	

* p < .05.
*** p < .001.

Counselors in the experimental group were reassessed six months after completion of the treatment manual implementation period to determine if they continued to use the manual over an extended period of time, after the completion of the active opinion leader training and consultation. Results suggested that over half of counselors in the experimental group were still using the treatment manual, and 81% reported using the manual in the past six months. Almost all of the counselors (97%) indicated that they planned to use the treatment manual in the future.

Changes in Counselor Practices, Attitudes, and Knowledge

Outcomes related to counselor practice behaviors, attitudes, and knowledge are presented in Table 3. The experimental and comparison groups did not differ on any of the baselines scores related to practices, attitudes, or knowledge. Comparative analyses of group changes over time indicated significant results for the CDTPS, $F(1, 54) = 5.88$, $p < .05$, with counselors in the experimental group showing greater positive change than the comparison sample in use of specialized and evidenced-based treatment practices with clients who have co-occurring disorders.

Analyses of counselor attitudes related to co-occurring disorders were complicated by the fact that both groups scored near the upper limit of the CDTAS. It was therefore difficult to detect group differences in changes over time, due to the attenuated range of scores. Over time, scores on the CDTAS increased slightly, but not significantly for the experimental group, and stayed about the same for the comparison group. Both the experimental and comparison groups were found to have slightly greater knowledge related to co-occurring disorders over time, as reflected by scores on the CODKT, although no significant group differences were detected.

Significant group differences were detected in the amount of time per week that counselors engaged in discussions with coworkers regarding clients who have co-occurring disorders, $F(1, 53) = 4.04$, $p < .05$; with the experimental group indicating an increase in this activity over time, while the comparison group reported a decrease in this activity. Although the results were not significant, counselors in the experimental group indicated a slight increase in the amount of time spent each week discussing co-occurring disorders in group treatment settings, while the comparison group reported a slight decrease in time allocated to these discussions. Weekly hours spent working with clients who have co-oc-

TABLE 3. Changes over time in co-occurring disorders treatment (CDT) practices, attitudes, knowledge, and time allocation by group

	Experimental Group (n = 43)		Comparison Group (n = 28)		
	Baseline M *(SD)*	Post-Imp. M *(SD)*	Baseline M *(SD)*	Post-Imp. M *(SD)*	Significance
CDT-Practices	3.30 (0.60)	3.58 (0.39)	3.35 (0.54)	3.33 (0.54)	F(1,54) = 5.88*
CDT-Attitudes	3.84 (0.49)	3.98 (0.55)	4.07 (0.51)	4.01 (0.49)	F(1,59) = 0.53
CDT Knowledge	29.51 (4.97)	32.00 (5.02)	30.07 (6.60)	31.26 (5.19)	F(1,60) = 3.13
Weekly Time Allocation: Hours working with clients who have co-occurring disorders	22.84 (15.20)	23.88 (16.42)	16.25 (14.08)	16.20 (15.64)	F(1,46) = 0.53
Minutes discussing co-occurring disorders in groups	107.25 (128.92)	141.61 (142.11)	136.86 (197.42)	120.95 (170.26)	F(1,43) = 0.21
Hours discussing clients who have co-occurring disorders with coworkers	5.08 (7.02)	8.28 (12.43)	6.74 (9.98)	3.48 (5.20)	F(1,53) = 4.04*

Note. Baseline scores, age, gender, and educational level served as covariates for each analysis of covariance.
* $p < .05$.

curring disorders did not change markedly among either group of counselors.

Counselors in the experimental group were reassessed at six months post-implementation, to assess the durability of changes in practice behaviors, attitudes, and knowledge relating to co-occurring disorders. As indicated in Table 4, repeated measures analyses of variance were performed on the practices, attitudes, and knowledge variables across the three time periods examined: (1) baseline, (2) post-implementation, and (3) six-month follow-up. Significant improvement in practice behaviors among the experimental group counselors was detected over time, based on findings from the CDTPS, $F(2,29) = 6.19$, $p < .01$. These practice behaviors included referral for co-occurring disorders treatment services (e.g., for medication consultation), evidence-based co-occurring disorders treatment practices (e.g., use of specialized manuals), and

TABLE 4. Experimental group changes over time in co-occurring disorders treatment (CDT) practices, attitudes, and knowledge

	Baseline M (SD)	Post-Imp. M (SD)	6-Month Follow-Up M (SD)	Significance
CDT-Practices	3.26 (0.63)[a]	3.52 (0.36)[b]	3.57 (0.46)[b]	$F(2,29) = 6.19^{**}$
CDT-Attitudes	3.82 (0.54)[a]	4.03 (0.55)[b]	3.91 (0.50)[ab]	$F(2,30) = 3.37^{*}$
CDT Knowledge	30.30 (4.53)[a]	31.90 (5.33)[b]	32.70 (4.68)[b]	$F(2,28) = 6.50^{**}$

Note. Significance was evaluated with repeated measures analyses of variance. Mean values with different superscript labels (i.e., "a" and "b") within each row reflect significant differences. Mean values within each row with similar superscript labels do not reflect significant differences, whereas "ab" indicates that the mean score is not significantly different from either the baseline or post-implementation score.

$^{*} p < .05.$
$^{**} p < .01.$

assessment of co-occurring disorders. Follow-up paired t-tests indicated that practice behaviors related to co-occurring disorders significantly improved from baseline to post-implementation, and then remained at about the same level over the six-month follow-up period.

Findings from the CDTAS measure of counselor attitudes were quite similar to those obtained from the CDTPS. Significant improvement in attitudes was detected over time, based on findings from the CDTAS, $F(2,30) = 3.37$, p < .05. As with the CDTPS, the pattern of CDTAS scores indicated that attitudes related to co-occurring disorders significantly improved from baseline to post-implementation, followed by slight, non-significant reductions over the six-month follow-up period. Counselors in the experimental group also demonstrated significant improvement over time in their knowledge of co-occurring disorders and of co-occurring disorders treatment, $F(2,28) = 6.50$, p < .01, based on CODKT scores. Knowledge increased significantly from baseline to post-implementation, with scores improving only slightly during the six-month follow-up period.

DISCUSSION

There is growing recognition that more aggressive efforts are needed to bridge the gap between practitioners, researchers, and policymakers in order to expedite the implementation of evidence-based practices,[1] particularly in substance abuse treatment and other health-related settings.[2,11,32] The current study examined the influence of peer opinion leaders' facilitation of structured training and consultation activities on substance abuse counselors' implementation of an evidence-based co-occurring disorders treatment manual. Although opinion leaders have been hailed as important change agents in disseminating evidence-based practices in health care settings,[23,24,26] this study was the first of its kind to assess the impact of opinion leaders' technology transfer activities within community-based substance abuse treatment programs.

Implementation of Evidence-Based Practices

Findings from the study indicate that substance abuse treatment counselors uniformly implemented an evidence-based treatment manual over a period of three months, when provided the opinion leader-facilitated structured training and consultation activities. In contrast, only 19% of the counselors from the comparison group implemented the treatment manual during the three-month period, who received only a general training workshop related to co-occurring disorders and were mailed a copy of the treatment manual. The study found that there was sustained implementation of the treatment manual among 48% of counselors in the experimental group who were examined at the end of the three-month implementation period. Among this same group of counselors, 52% had sustained implementation of the manual at the six-month follow-up period. Only 19% of counselors in the comparison group continued to use the manual at the end of the three-month implementation period. Additionally, the overwhelming majority of counselors in the experimental group reported that they planned to use the treatment manual in the future. Surprisingly, over half of the comparison sample also reported plans to use the manual in the future.

The primary intent of the study was to examine implementation patterns of the treatment manual among experimental and comparison groups. However, the opinion leader-facilitated training and consultation also appeared to increase the frequency of several desirable clinical practices used with clients who have co-occurring disorders, including use of evidence-based practices related to referral, assessment, and co-occurring disorders treatment. Moreover, the opinion leader-facilitated intervention was associated with increased counselor communication with co-workers regarding co-occurring disorders issues.

The greatest impact of opinion leader-facilitated training and consultation interventions appears to be during supervised implementation of evidence-based practices. Findings indicated that there was approximately 50% attrition in counselor use of the evidence-based practice materials by the end of the three-month implementation period. However, over a subsequent six-month follow-up period there was very little additional attrition in use of the evidence-based practice. Moreover, counselors demonstrated continued interest and enthusiasm in the evidence-based protocols at the end of the follow-up period, and planned to use these materials in their future clinical work.

Although there were modest positive changes in counselors' attitudes in working with clients who have co-occurring disorders, following counselors' exposure to the opinion leader-facilitated intervention, no significant group differences were found between the experimental and comparison samples. Similarly, counselors who received the opinion leader-facilitated intervention experienced modest gains in co-occurring disorders knowledge acquisition during the three-month implementation period, although these were not significantly different from the comparison group. Knowledge levels continued to rise in the experimental group during the six-month follow-up period, indicating that counselors may have learned more about co-occurring disorders after they had experience in implementing the manual and in providing treatment for co-occurring disorders. It should be noted that the samples consisted of highly experienced counselors (averaging from 5-12 years of work in the adult services area), who scored in the higher range of the baseline attitudinal and knowledge acquisition measures. This attenuated range of scores in outcome measures diminished the likelihood of obtaining significant results on these measures. Administration of the counselor attitude scale over time may have yielded a more pronounced pattern of results among less experienced counselors.

Outcome findings from the study support the effectiveness of opinion leaders in facilitating technology transfer within substance abuse treatment settings, particularly when opinion leaders are actively engaged in providing ongoing training and consultation with peer counselors. These findings are consistent with other studies examining outcomes related to use of opinion leaders in health care settings,[19,23-25] and with investigations examining use of interactive peer training techniques to stimulate technology transfer.[5,7]

The current study indicates that substance abuse treatment agencies that are interested in durable, widespread technology transfer of evidence-based practices should consider identifying and recruiting peer opinion leaders to assist in these efforts. The identification of opinion leaders through network analysis techniques is neither time consuming nor costly,[19,32] and could enhance treatment providers' abilities to introduce and sustain new treatment approaches. Moreover, opinion leaders represent a hidden and often untapped resource within treatment agencies, as a significant proportion of opinion leaders are not currently serving as clinical supervisors within their organizations.[32] Pairing opinion leaders and clinical supervisors may potentially assist substance abuse treatment agencies to expedite the technology transfer process.

Limitations of the Study

Among the limitations to the current study is the relatively small sample size of opinion leaders and counselors examined. The generalizability of findings is also limited by the geographic region and urban location of the participating treatment agencies, the ethnic/demographic and vocational background of counselors, and the focus on substance abuse treatment. In this regard, it would be helpful to determine whether the same pattern of results is replicated in other geographic areas, in rural settings, with counselors of different ethnic and demographic backgrounds, with less experienced counselors, and in other health care and social service settings. Although the experimental and comparison groups were not equivalent in age, gender, and education, analyses conducted for the study controlled for these variables.

Another concern in interpreting results from the study is that the intervention examined was multi-faceted, and included not only the counselor's exposure to peer opinion leaders, but also their involvement in a structured regimen of training and consultation. Thus, it is somewhat difficult to calibrate the independent effects of these variables (i.e., counselor involvement with opinion leaders, counselor involvement in structured training and consultation activities) on the outcomes obtained in the study. For example, it is unclear whether training and consultation provided by non-opinion leaders would have similar outcomes related to implementation of the treatment manual. Although several potential mediating variables (e.g., organizational support and readiness for change) were assessed, it is difficult to gauge the effects of the treatment agency's administrative support for the study on counselors' implementation of the treatment manual.

Despite providing clear information to opinion leaders in this study regarding the beginning and ending dates of the treatment manual implementation period, it is unclear to what extent opinion leaders' continued to play a significant role in supervising and mentoring peer counselors in issues related to co-occurring disorders treatment, and thereby potentially influencing them to continue to use the manual during the six-month follow-up period. In addition, extensive follow-up research was not conducted to determine the level of administrative support provided for continuation of the treatment manual. In this regard, it would be useful to examine the effects of different levels of administrative support and of opinion leader involvement during extended follow-up periods on technology transfer outcomes, and to identify the most important types of counselor contact and the intensity or frequency of contact that are needed to sustain technology transfer efforts.

AUTHORS NOTE

This study was conducted as part of the Center for Substance Abuse Treatment (CSAT) Practice Improvement Collaborative (PIC) initiative. Several staff from participating treatment and criminal justice agencies were instrumental in helping to coordinate the PIC research efforts, including Betty Buchan, at Operation PAR, Inc., Liz Harden at DACCO, Inc., Michelle Smith at ACTS, Inc., and Joel Pietsch at the Hillsborough County Sheriff's Office. The authors would also like to recognize the leadership of Fran Cotter and Sue Rohrer from the Center for Substance Abuse Treatment for their coordination of the PIC network grant program.

Funding for this project was supported by the Substance Abuse & Mental Health Services Administration, Center for Substance Abuse Treatment, Practice Improvement Collaborative (PIC) network grant #: 5 UD1 TI12662-03.

REFERENCES

1. Lamb S, Greenlick M, McCarty D. Bridging the gap between practice and research: Forging partnerships with community-based drug and alcohol treatment. Washington, DC: National Academy Press, 1998.

2. McLellan AT. Technology transfer and the treatment of addiction: What can research offer practice? J SubAbuseTreat. 2002; 22:169-170.

3. Galanter M, Kleber HD. Textbook of substance abuse treatment. Washington, DC: American Psychiatric Press, 1999.

4. Lowinson JH, Ruiz P, Millman RB, Langrod JG. Substance abuse: A comprehensive textbook–3rd edition. Baltimore: Williams & Wilkens, 1997.

5. Backer TE, David SL, Saucy G. Introduction. In Backer TE, David SL, Saucy G (Eds.). Reviewing the behavioral science knowledge base on technology transfer. NIDA Research Monograph #155. Rockville, MD: National Institute on Drug Abuse, 1995.

6. Sorensen JL, Rawson RA, Guydish J, Zweben JE (Eds.). Drug abuse treatment through collaboration: Practice and research partnerships that work. Washington, DC: American Psychological Association, 2003.

7. Backer TE. The failure of success: Challenges of disseminating effective substance abuse prevention programs. J Comm Psych. 2000; 28(3):363-373.

8. Hyde PS, Falls K, Morris JA, Schoenwald, SK (Eds.). Turning knowledge into practice: A manual for behavioral health administrators and practitioners about under-

standing and implementing evidence-based practices. Boston, MA: The Technical Assistance Collaborative, 2003.

9. Cabana ME, Rand CS, Powe NR, Wu AW, Wilson MH, Abboud PE, Rubin HR. Why don't physicians follow clinical practice guidelines?: A framework for improvement. J Am Med Assoc. 1999; 282(15):1458-1465.

10. Marinelli-Casey P, Doomier CP, Rawson RA. The gap between research and practice in substance abuse treatment. Psyctric Srvcs. 2002; 53(8):984-987.

11. Simpson DD. A conceptual framework for transferring research to practice. J Sub Abuse Treat. 2002; 22:171-182.

12. Gerstein D, Harwood H. Treating drug problems: Volume 1. Institute of Medicine, Washington, DC: National Academy Press, 1990.

13. Schmidt F, Taylor TK. Putting empirically supported treatments into practice: Lessons learned in a children's mental health center. Prof Psych Res Pract. 2002; 33(5):483-489.

14. Locock L, Dopson S, Chambers D, Gabbay J. Understanding the role of opinion leaders in improving clinical effectiveness. Soc Sci Med. 2001; 53:745-757.

15. Davis DA, Thomson MA, Oxman AD, Haynes B. Changing physician performance: A systematic review of the effect of continuing medical education strategies. J Am Med Assoc. 1995; 274(9):700-705.

16. Rothenberg R, Koplan JP, Cutler C, Hillman AL. Changing pediatric practice in a changing medical environment: Factors that influence what physicians do. Ped Annals. 1998; 27(4):241-250.

17. Rogers EM. Diffusion of innovations, 5th edition. New York: Free Press, 2003.

18. Rogers EM, Kinkaid D. Communication networks: A new paradigm for research. New York: Free Press, 1981.

19. Valente TW, Davis RL. Accelerating the diffusion of innovations using opinion leaders. Annals. 1999; 566:55-67.

20. Scott J. Network analysis: A handbook, 2nd edition. Newbury Park: Sage, 2000.

21. Valente TW. Methods for identifying opinion leaders. Unpublished manuscript, 2000.

22. Wasserman S, Faust K. Social network analysis: Methods and applications. New York: Cambridge University Press, 1994.

23. Kelly JA, St. Lawrence JS, Diaz YE, Stevenson LY, Hauth AC, Brasfield TL, Kalichman SC, Smith JE, Andrew ME. HIV risk behavior reduction following intervention with key opinion leaders of population: An experimental analysis. Am J Pub Health. 1991; 81(2):168-171.

24. Lomas J, Enkin M, Anderson GM, Hannah WJ, Vayda E, Singer J. Opinion leaders vs. audit and feedback to implement practice guidelines. J Am Med Assoc. 1991; 265(17):2202-2207.

25. Sorensen JL, Clark WW. A field-based dissemination component in a drug abuse research center. In TE Backer, SL David (Eds.), Reviewing the behavioral science knowledge base on technology transfer, 186-197. Rockville, MD: NIH Publication No. 95-4035; National Institutes of Health, 1995.

26. Soumerai SB, McLaughlin TJ, Gurwitz JH, Guadagnoli E, Hauptman PJ, Borbas C, Morris N, McLaughlin B, Gao X, Willison DJ, Asinger R, Gobel F. Effect of

local medical opinion leaders on quality of care for acute myocardial infarction. J Am Med Assoc. 1998; 279(17):1358-1363.

27. Gingiss PL, Gottlieb NH, Brink SG. Measuring cognitive characteristics associated with adoption and implementation of health innovations in schools. Am J Health Prom. 1994; 8:294-301.

28. Rohrbach LA, Graham JW, Hansen WB. Diffusion of a school-based substance abuse prevention program: Predictors of program implementation. Prev Medicine. 1993; 22:237-260.

29. Sobol DF, Rohrbach LA, Dent CW, Gleason L, Brannon BR, Johnson CA, Flay BR. The integrity of smoking prevention curriculum delivery. Health Ed Research. 1989; 4:59-67.

30. Young RL, DeMoor C, Wildey MB, Gully S, Hovell MF, Elder JP. Correlates of health facilitator performance in a tobacco use prevention program: Implications for recruitment. J School Health. 1990; 60:463-467.

31. Mueser KT, Fox L. Stage-wise family treatment for dual disorders treatment manual. Concord, NH: New Hampshire-Dartmouth Psychiatric Research Center, 1998.

32. Moore KA, Peters RH, Hills HA, LeVasseur JB, Rich AR, Hunt WM, Young MS, Valente TW. Characteristics of Opinion Leaders in Community-Based Substance Abuse Treatment Agencies. Am J Drug Alc Abuse. 2004; 30(1):1-17.

33. Moore KA, Matthews C, Hunt WM, Fox L, Mueser KT. Co-occurring disorders treatment manual. Tampa, FL: Louis de la Parte Florida Mental Health Institute, 2001.

34. Lehman WEK, Greener JM, Simpson DD. Assessing organizational readiness for change. J Sub Abuse Treat. 2002; 22:197-209.

The Relationship
Between Addictions Counselors'
Clinical Orientations
and Their Readiness
to Change Counseling Techniques

Paul J. Toriello, RhD
Stephanie Roahen-Harrison, MPH
Janet Rice, PhD
Richard Ager, PhD
Edward V. Morse, PhD
Patricia Morse, PhD
Linton Carney, JD
Patricia J. Kissinger, PhD

Paul J. Toriello is affiliated with the Louisiana State University Health Sciences Center, Department of Rehabilitation Counseling.

Stephanie Roahen-Harrison, Janet Rice, and Patricia J. Kissinger are affiliated with Tulane University, School of Public Health & Tropical Medicine.

Richard Ager is affiliated with Tulane University, School of Social Work.

Edward V. Morse is affiliated with Tulane University, Department of Pediatrics.

Patricia Morse is affiliated with the Louisiana State University Health Sciences Center, Department of Psychiatry.

Linton Carney is affiliated with AIDSLaw of Louisiana, New Orleans.

Address correspondence to: Paul J. Toriello, RhD, Department of Rehabilitation Counseling, LSUHSC, 1900 Gravier Street, Box G6-2, Room 8C-1, New Orleans, LA 70112 (E-mail: ptorie@lsuhsc.edu).

[Haworth co-indexing entry note]: "The Relationship Between Addictions Counselors' Clinical Orientations and Their Readiness to Change Counseling Techniques." Toriello, Paul J. et al. Co-published simultaneously in *Journal of Addictive Diseases* (The Haworth Medical Press, an imprint of The Haworth Press, Inc.) Vol. 24, Supplement No. 1, 2005, pp. 75-92; and: *Implementing Evidence-Based Practices for Treatment of Alcohol and Drug Disorders* (ed: Eldon Edmundson, Jr., and Dennis McCarty) The Haworth Medical Press, an imprint of The Haworth Press, Inc., 2005, pp. 75-92. Single or multiple copies of this article are available for a fee from The Haworth Document Delivery Service [1-800-HAWORTH, 9:00 a.m. - 5:00 p.m. (EST). E-mail address: docdelivery@haworthpress.com].

Available online at http://www.haworthpress.com/web/JAD
doi:10.1300/J069v24S01_05

SUMMARY. We examined the relationship between addiction counselors' clinical orientations and their readiness to change counseling techniques. Participants (n = 212) completed the Short Understanding of Substance Abuse Scale, a modified version of the Treatment Process Rating Questionnaire, and a modified version of the Stages of Change Readiness and Treatment Eagerness Scale. Cluster analysis suggested that participants endorsed either a "traditional," "non-traditional," or "multiform" clinical orientation. Characteristics of each group are described. Readiness to change was higher among women and individuals who were not African-American. Clinical orientation was not associated with readiness to change counseling techniques. Implications for addictions counseling practice, training, and research are discussed. *[Article copies available for a fee from The Haworth Document Delivery Service: 1-800-HAWORTH. E-mail address: <docdelivery@haworthpress.com> Website: <http://www.HaworthPress.com> © 2005 by The Haworth Press, Inc. All rights reserved.]*

KEYWORDS. Addictions counselor, clinical orientation, readiness to change

INTRODUCTION

A challenge for the addictions treatment field is to build a treatment system that is based on current scientific evidence.[1] Integral to this system is the dissemination and adoption of "evidence-based practices." Evidence-based practices consist of conceptually sound and internally consistent interventions that, through comprehensive implementation and evaluation, are linked to positive treatment outcomes.[2] Examples of evidence-based practices include motivational interventions (e.g., Motivational Interviewing[3]), cognitive behavioral therapies (e.g., Cognitive Behavioral Coping Skills Training[4]), and pharmacological interventions (e.g., Naltrexone[5]). Even though manuals and technical assistance are available to support evidence-based practices dissemination and adoption, addictions counselors are not adopting evidence-based practices in a widespread manner.[1,6-9] Several researchers have suggested that examination of addictions counselors' variables may explain the lack of evidence-based practices adoption.[10-12]

Clinical orientations (i.e., beliefs about addiction etiology and the counseling techniques used to counsel clients with addiction), for example, may impact readiness to change counseling techniques. Counselors may endorse a range of clinical orientations from traditional to contemporary.[8,13] Clinical orientation complexity may predict willingness to adopt evidence-based practices. As evidence-based practices continue to evolve to accommodate new evidence, an understanding of this relationship will support educators and supervisors as they work with counselors to cope with the pressure of adopting incessantly evolving evidence-based practices.[1] The purpose of this study was to conduct an initial, exploratory examination of the influence of clinical orientations on counselor readiness to change counseling techniques.

Studies that examine clinical orientations suggest a continuum of orientations from traditional to contemporary.[13-17] Counselors with traditional clinical orientations support a disease model and moralistic beliefs about addiction etiology and counseling techniques. Those with contemporary orientations, conversely, support client-centered and/or cognitive-behavioral beliefs about addiction etiology and counseling techniques and reflect evidence-based practices.[13] Counselors may also endorse a mixture of traditional and contemporary beliefs and techniques. (Table 1 presents a list of typically traditional and contemporary beliefs and techniques. Traditional items are noted with a "T" and contemporary items are noted with a "C.") Morgenstern and McCrady concluded that the traditional orientation was "evolving into a more complex treatment approach integrating the therapeutic aspects of other models."[16,18,19] Thombs and Osborn furthered this thought and concluded that managed care's emphasis on counselor certification and licensure standards encourages a more contemporary (i.e., evidence-based) orientation.[13] However, Moyers and Miller reported that the traditional orientation had changed little since inception during the 1950s.[17] Instead of drawing conclusions on the change or lack of change in clinical orientations over time or in regard to different pressures, a more useful strategy may be to assess change or lack of change among counselors who endorse a particular clinical orientation. Indeed, Thombs and Osborn suggested that counselors with different orientations "may vary in their openness to new clinical practices."[13] A good beginning point for examining this relationship may be with the concept of readiness to change.

Readiness to change is most often linked to Prochaska and DiClementes' seminal work on the Transtheoretical Model of the stages of change.[20,21] According to the model, behavior change progresses through a series of distinct stages. Stages include precontemplation (not thinking about change), contemplation (thinking about change), preparation (intending to make a change), action (behavioral change), and maintenance (sustaining behavioral change). In their critique, Littell

TABLE 1. Cluster Means by Clinical Orientation and Item

Item (abbreviated)	Cluster Means			Post-hoc Comparisons		
	1-Traditional	2-Non-traditional	3-Multiform	1 vs. 2	2 vs. 3	1 vs. 3
Help client accept addiction is a disease (T)	0.293	−0.761	0.439	*	*	
Reduce client denial (T)	0.289	−0.689	0.401	*	*	
Clients must accept powerlessness over drugs (T)	0.373	−0.723	0.549	*	*	
Every addict is one hit away from a total relapse (T)	0.235	−0.764	0.635	*	*	*
People can be born addicts (T)	0.076	−0.196	0.207		*	
Once an addict, always an addict (T)	−0.223	−0.192	0.461		*	*
Addiction is progressive even during abstinence (T)	0.106	−0.533	0.453	*	*	
Only two options for an addict: abstinence or death (T)	0.018	−0.723	0.664	*	*	*
Addicts cannot control their use (T)	0.105	−0.708	0.547	*	*	*
Addicts have distinct personality (T)	0.021	−0.560	0.528	*	*	*
An unmotivated addict cannot be helped (T)	−0.230	−0.112	0.431		*	*
Addicts fail to recover in because they are in denial (T)	−0.169	−0.355	0.488		*	*
Denial is part of the personality of the drug addict (T)	0.286	−0.554	0.358	*	*	
Addicts should never receive psychiatric medications (T)	0.275	−0.227	−0.017	*		
Increase knowledge of religious practices for clients (T)	0.371	−0.382	0.083	*	*	
Facilitate a faith-based experience for clients (T)	0.259	−0.524	0.262	*	*	
Facilitate a community where clients help clients (T)	0.031	−0.349	0.326		*	
Facilitate intense interactions within a client community (T)	−0.002	−0.368	0.394		*	*
Provide client with psychiatric medications (C)	0.138	−0.322	0.222	*	*	
Society/culture influences addiction development (C)	−0.912	0.188	0.369	*		*
Clients' environments influences addiction (C)	−0.841	0.093	0.450	*	*	*
Addiction is partly caused by a dysfunctional family (C)	−0.675	−0.037	0.501	*	*	*

	Cluster Means			Post-hoc Comparisons		
Item (abbreviated)	1-Traditional	2-Non-traditional	3-Multiform	1 vs. 2	2 vs. 3	1 vs. 3
Addiction is partly caused learning use from others (C)	−0.657	0.055	0.430	*	*	*
Addiction is caused by psychological problems (C)	−0.842	0.171	0.384	*		*
Some "problem drinkers" are not alcoholic (C)	−0.293	0.296	−0.127	*		*
Facilitate self-discrepancy in clients (C)	0.225	−0.379	0.139	*	*	
Increase clients' emotional involvement in treatment (C)	0.229	−0.332	0.107	*	*	

*$p < .05$.

and Girvin found that since 1990, over 175 empirical studies examined readiness to change and the stages of change model.[22] A majority of these studies examined health behavior changes with various human service clientele.[23] However, the application of the stages of change model to professionals and their professional behavior changes has not been comprehensively examined.

Examining readiness to change among professionals progressing through work-related changes seems to be a promising approach for several reasons. First, the stages of change model can be applied to any problem behavior regardless if individuals are involved in treatment or not.[22] Counselors, for example, may react to expectations for change in counseling techniques with resistance followed by ambivalence, then action, etc., which suggests that this behavior might progress through change stages. Scales have been developed for assessing readiness to change but the scales have not been applied to change in counseling techniques.[22] Our study represents an initial examination of the relationship between clinical orientations and readiness to change counseling techniques and an assessment of characteristics that facilitate or impede change. Results from this study would support clinical supervisors facilitating their supervisees' adoption of evidence-based practice with information on the impact clinical orientation has on that process. Moreover, results may benefit educators when exposing students to various addictions counseling clinical orientations. Finally, researchers would have an initial platform for future studies examining clinical orientation and readiness to change. Due to the initial, exploratory nature of this study, two research questions guided the analysis:

- How do the clinical orientations of a sample of counselors compare and contrast to those found in previous studies?
- What is the relationship of counselors' clinical orientations to their readiness to change counseling techniques?

METHOD

Participants and Procedure

This study was funded by a Center for Substance Abuse Treatment grant awarded to the New Orleans Practice Improvement Collaborative of the Council on Alcohol and Drug Abuse for Greater New Orleans in 2000 and was approved by the Tulane University Institutional Review Board for research involving human subjects. Recruitment letters were sent to all substance abuse agencies, licensed social workers, and board certified addiction counselors in the area. Follow-up phone calls and visits were made to agencies. With each contact, requests were made for additional individuals who might be interested in participating. We accepted individuals into the study if they planned to live in southern Louisiana for at least the next year, at least 10% of their caseload was substance-involved adolescents (ages 13-18) or incarcerated/post-incarcerated individuals, and they were not proficient with Motivational Interviewing (determined by responses to a series of questions). If the individual did not have an active caseload but was an administrator of a substance abuse agency, s/he was allowed to participate. Our recruitment efforts lead to a sample of 316 participants, all of which gave written consent to participate in the study.

Prior to interventions to facilitate adoption of motivational enhancement therapy, clinical orientation, readiness to change counseling techniques, and key demographics were assessed. An interdisciplinary team of experienced researchers developed the instrumentation and pre-tested the survey with counselors who were not participating in the study. Participants received $10 for completing and returning the survey. Multiple attempts were made to achieve an adequate responses rate. Out of the 316 participants mailed surveys, a total of 247 returned their surveys for a response rate of 78%. Thirty-five participants were removed from the analysis due to missing data, leaving a sample size of 212 for this analysis.

More than two-thirds (68%) of the 212 respondents were women. Respondents ranged in age from 23 to 71 years (M = 42.4; SD = 11.0).

Most (57%) were African American, and 40% were Caucasian. Over half (53%) of the participating counselors had a master's or doctoral degree, one in five (22%) had a bachelor's degree, and one in four (25%) were not college graduates. Participants' mean years of experience was 7.4 years (standard deviation = 7.0). Approximately 24% of the respondents considered themselves to be a recovering addict and/or alcoholic. The sample included 17% state board-certified addiction counselors; 20% of the sample was "counselors in training" for this certification. Other professional credentials included, but were not limited to, licensed clinical social worker (17%), licensed counselor (6%), and licensed nurse (6%).

Measures

Short Understanding of Substance Abuse Scale. In building upon the work of Miller and Moyers,' Humphreys et al. assessed the reliability and validity of a modified version of their Understanding of Alcoholism Scale with a more representative sample.[14,24] They reduced the number of items to 19 and modified the items to assess beliefs about substance abuse in general as opposed to solely alcoholism. The resulting instrument demonstrated both convergent and discriminant validity, as well as internal consistency coefficients greater than .60. The nineteen items measure beliefs about substance abuse. Participants responded from 1 (strongly disagree) to 5 (strongly agree) on the extent to which they agreed with each belief about substance abuse.

Modified Treatment Processes Rating Questionnaire. Morgenstern and McCrady developed the Treatment Processes Rating Questionnaire to assess the addictions counseling processes that counselors deem essential.[16] The 35 items assess processes related to the disease model, behavioral techniques, general psychotherapy, and pharmacological interventions. Ogborne, Wild, Braun, and Newton-Taylor reported alphas of .8 or higher on all domains.[25] To increase response rate, the number of items was reduced to 12. Five substance abuse counseling experts reached a consensus on two items from each of the four models that best represented the overall philosophy of the respective model. Additionally, these experts generated, via literature review, four new items related to counseling processes germane to a Therapeutic Community model (two items) and a Faith-Based model (two items). Items were revised to address both alcohol and drug counseling processes without changing the original content.[13] Also, we changed overly complex words to enhance readability (e.g., "affective" was changed to "emotional" and "provisional" was changed to "temporary"). Participants rated the 12-items from -3 (harmful) to $+3$ (helpful) on how helpful they consider each process.

Readiness to Change Counseling Techniques Scale. To measure participants' readiness to change counseling techniques, we developed a scale based on six items from Miller and Tonigans' Stages of Change Readiness and Treatment Eagerness Scale (SOCRATES).[26] Based on the stages of change model, they developed the SOCRATES to assess readiness to change in alcohol abusers. Different from other readiness to change instruments that assess readiness to change in general, the 19-item SOCRATES poses questions about readiness to change alcohol use and has test-retest reliabilities greater than .80. Using the SOCRATES as the framework, six items were translated to assess readiness to change counseling techniques. For example, we translated "I'm not just thinking about changing drug use, I'm already doing something about it" into "I'm not just thinking about changing my counseling techniques, I'm already doing something about it." Thus, participants rated their agreement with the six such statements from 1 (strongly disagree) to 5 (strongly agree). We performed a factor analysis to ensure that the variables retained from the original SOCRATES measured one construct representing readiness to change counseling techniques. The principal components extraction method was used with a varimax rotation, specifying retention of eigenvalues greater than one. An item was considered to load on a factor if the loading was at least 0.40 for that factor, and less than 0.40 for any other factors. We estimated the internal consistency of the scale using Cronbach's alpha coefficient. The results of the factor analysis showed that the six items measured a single, unidimensional construct measuring readiness to change counseling techniques. Only one factor was extracted with an eigenvalue greater than one, representing 63% of the total variance. Factor loadings ranged from 0.61 to 0.88. Chronbach's alpha was 0.87, representing a reliable measure of the construct.

RESULTS

Cluster Analysis

We used SPSS version 11.0 cluster procedures to group participants according to their responses on the 19 Short Understanding of Substance Abuse Scale items and the 12 modified Treatment Process Rating Questionnaire items. With the number of clusters set *a priori* at three (based on Thombs and Osborns' findings) and standardizing scores from the instruments, hierarchical cluster analysis determined the initial cluster centers of the 31 items using Ward's method and the squared Euclidian distance coefficients to measure center proximity.[13,27] Using the cluster centers from the hierarchical analysis, we then performed a non-hierarchical, *k*-means cluster analysis to specify the best three-cluster solution. Results revealed that 27 out of the 31 items significantly differentiated cluster membership ($p < .05$). We named each cluster based on their clinical orientation characteristics: "traditional," "non-traditional," and "multiform." Table 1 contains cluster profiles which include the cluster means of each cluster on each of the 27 items, as well as results from post-hoc comparisons (Tukey) of these means; traditional items are noted with a "T" and contemporary items are noted with a "C."

The smallest cluster consisted of 53 (25%) participants. Labeled traditional, this group endorsed consistent, albeit modest, support for traditional beliefs and processes. Consistently, this group strongly rejected contemporary beliefs. Demographically, of the traditional counselors, 81.1% were female, 63.5% were African American, with 40.4% possessing a graduate degree and 30.2% in recovery from addiction. The average age was 43.7 years and the average years of experience were 8.9. The next largest cluster consisted of 79 (37%) participants. Labeled non-traditional, this group moderately supported the contemporary beliefs that the traditional counselors strongly rejected and strongly rejected traditional beliefs and processes. Of the non-traditional counselors, 60.8% were female, 38% were African American, with 75.6% possessing a graduate degree and 11.4% in recovery from addiction. The average age was 43 years and the average years of experience was 6.5. The largest cluster consisted of 80 (38%) participants. Labeled multiform, this group strongly supported a broad range of both traditional and contemporary beliefs. The only beliefs they rejected were "some problem drinkers are not alcoholic" and "addicts should never receive psychiatric medications." Of the multiform counselors, 66.3% were female, 71.3% were African American, with 40% possessing a graduate degree and 31.3% in recovery from addiction. Their average age was 40.9 years and the average years of experience were 7.6.

Validation of the Three-Cluster Solution

We attempted to validate our cluster solution with significance tests of variables (a) not used in the clustering procedures and (b) found to associate with clinical orientation in previous studies.[13-15,17] First, we conducted a discriminant function analysis with gender, race (African American vs. non-African American), education level (less than bachelor's, bachelor's, and graduate), years of experience (5 years or less vs. more than 5 years), licensure status (yes/no), and recovery status (yes/no) as the independent variables and cluster membership as the dependent variable. Results revealed one significant function (Eigenvalue = .180, canonical correlation = .391, $p < .001$), with education level (structure coefficient = .830) and race (structure coefficient = −.732) discriminating non-traditional counselors from traditional and multiform counselors. This function accounted for 96% of the variance in the clusters. A second function (Eigenvalue = .008, canonical correlation = .087, $p = .224$), albeit non-significant, emerged from the analysis that discriminated traditional counselors from non-traditional and multiform counselors. This function accounted for 4% of the variance in the clusters.

Next, we investigated bivariate and multivariate relationships between the variables used in the discriminant analysis and the two orientation groups discriminated by the discriminant function analysis (i.e., non-traditional versus traditional/multiform combined). Table 2 shows that compared to traditional/multiform counselors, non-traditional counselors were significantly more likely to be male, non-African American, licensed, non-recovering, or have a graduate degree. Next, variables with p-values less than 0.20 were entered into a logistic regression. Everything remained significant except licensure status.

The Relationship Between Readiness to Change and Clinical Orientation

To examine the relationship between clinical orientations and readiness to change counseling techniques, we conducted a linear regression analysis with readiness to change counseling techniques as the dependent variable, measured by participants' total scores on the six readiness to change items. For independent variables, we included all variables into the model, including the two-group clinical orientation variable (see Table 3). Only gender and race were associated with readiness to change counseling techniques with $p \leq 0.05$: women and non-African Americans were likely to have higher scores on the readiness to change items. The mean score of these items was 22.7 (SD = 4.3, range 6-30). Finally, this model only explained 8% of the variance in readiness to change scores.

TABLE 2. Bivariate Analyses and Logistic Regression of Selected Variables by Clinical Orientation

	Non-Traditional (n = 79)		Traditional/Multiform (n = 133)		Unadjusted OR (95% CI)	Adjusted OR (95% CI)
	n	%	n	%		
Gender						
Female	48	(60.8)	96	(72.2)	1.00	1.00
Male	31	(39.2)	37	(27.8)	1.68 (0.93, 3.02)	2.24 (1.12, 4.50)*
Race						
Non-African American	49	(62.0)	42	(31.8)	1.00	1.00
African American	30	(38.0)	90	(68.2)	0.29 (0.16, 0.51)*	3.59 (1.78, 7.22)*
Education						
Less than Bachelor's degree	8	(10.3)	44	(33.3)	1.00	1.00
Bachelor's degree	11	(14.1)	35	(26.5)	1.73 (0.63, 4.76)	1.25 (0.42, 3.74)
Graduate degree	59	(75.6)	53	(40.2)	6.12 (2.64, 14.18)*	3.56 (1.32, 9.65)*
Recovery status						
Not in recovery	70	(88.6)	92	(69.2)	1.00	1.00
In recovery	9	(11.4)	41	(30.8)	0.29 (0.13, 0.63)*	0.28 (0.11, 0.75)*
Licensure						
Not licensed	55	(69.6)	110	(82.7)	1.00	1.00
Licensed	24	(30.4)	23	(17.3)	2.09 (1.08, 4.03)*	0.56 (0.24, 1.29)
Years of experience†						
5 years or less	41	(52.6)	68	(52.7)	1.00	-----
More than 5 years	37	(47.4)	61	(47.3)	1.01 (0.57, 1.77)	-----

*p-value < .05.
†Not entered into logistic regression.

DISCUSSION

Clinical Orientations

Like Thombs and Osborn, we set our cluster analysis procedures to specify a three-cluster solution, thus clustering our sample on three clinical orientations.[13] Referring to the clinical orientation continuum with

TABLE 3. Linear Regression of Readiness to Change Counseling Techniques (N = 205*)

	Beta Coefficient	Standard Error	t	p-value
Constant	24.28			
Gender (Male)	−1.78	0.68	−2.61	0.01
Race (African American)	−1.35	0.70	−1.94	0.05
Education				
Less than Bachelor's degree	−1.03	0.94	−1.10	0.27
Bachelor's degree	−0.43	0.87	−0.49	0.62
Graduate degree	1.00			
Non-Traditional orientation	0.34	0.70	0.48	0.63
In recovery	0.01	0.88	0.01	0.99
Licensed	−0.46	0.88	−0.52	0.60
Years of counseling experience	0.02	0.05	0.52	0.61

*Seven individuals were missing readiness to change scores.

traditional and contemporary orientations at the extremes, we labeled the clinical orientations found in our study based on where they fall on the continuum: "traditional" (cluster 1), "non-traditional" (cluster 2), and "multiform" (cluster 3).

Traditional Clinical Orientation. The traditional end of the continuum seems to best characterize 25% of our sample. Here, counselors endorsed beliefs and processes that reflect traditional beliefs and processes (e.g., help client accept that addiction is a disease and commit to Alcoholics Anonymous(AA)/Narcotics Anonymous (NA); reduce client denial). Of particular interest is that our traditional counselors, like Thombs and Osborns' "uniform" counselors, strongly rejected non-traditional or more contemporary processes and beliefs (e.g., addiction is partially caused by one's environment; underlying psychological issues can cause addiction; society/culture influences addiction; addiction is learned).[13] However, traditional counselors comprised only 25% of our sample as opposed to 56% of Thombs and Osborns' sample. As with previous studies, having lower education levels discriminated traditional counselors from other orientations. However, unlike previous studies we also found that being female discriminated a traditional orientation.

Non-Traditional Clinical Orientation. The contemporary end of the continuum seems to best characterize 37% of our sample. Here our participants, as well as those in previous studies, endorsed behavioral or other contemporary beliefs and processes, and strongly rejected traditional beliefs and processes. We labeled the portion of our sample at this end of the continuum non-traditional as opposed to contemporary because they did not seem to endorse a purely contemporary orientation. They strongly rejected traditional beliefs but did not endorse all contemporary beliefs. For example, they rejected the process of helping clients experience a discrepancy between their current self-image and ideal self-image (a process associated with Motivational Interviewing).[3] As with previous studies, having higher education levels discriminated non-traditional counselors from other orientations. Like Thombs and Osborn, we also found that being non-African American, non-recovering, or having a license discriminated a non-traditional orientation.[13] However, unlike previous studies, we also found that being male discriminated a non-traditional orientation.

Multiform Clinical Orientation. The middle area of the clinical orientation continuum seems to best characterize 38% of our sample. Like Thombs and Osborn, we labeled this group multiform because they strongly endorsed a wide range of beliefs and processes, both traditional and contemporary. Our multiform counselors rejected only two items (i.e., some problem drinkers are not alcoholic and addicts should never be given psychiatric medications). This suggests that multiform counselors fall in the middle of the continuum, not because they have moderate beliefs, but because they endorse extreme beliefs associated with both ends of the continuum. This pattern may explain why our cluster validation procedures did not discriminate multiform counselors from the other orientations. This is unlike Thombs and Osborn, who were able to discriminate multiform from non-traditional counselors.[13] For example, they found that multiform counselors were more likely to be African American with a bachelor's degree or less. However, like our study, Thombs and Osborn were not able to discriminate multiform from traditional counselors. This lack of discrimination may be due to the limited variables we used for our cluster validation analyses.

Relationship Between Clinical Orientation and Readiness to Change Counseling Techniques

Our results did not reveal a significant relationship between counselors' clinical orientations and their readiness to change counseling techniques. In fact, the sample as a whole indicated strong readiness to change counseling techniques by scoring well above the median score on the readiness to change items. However, the linear regression did reveal that women and non-African Americans exhibited higher readiness to change counseling techniques. Discussing these results is difficult as we could not find any previous studies examining this relationship. Lehman, Greener, and Simpson did find differences between agency staff and directors on perceived opportunities for professional growth (e.g., "you read about new techniques and treatment information each month" and "you do a good job of regularly updating and improving your skills") and adaptability (e.g., "you are willing to try new ideas even if some staff members are reluctant"), but they did not examine these variables in relation to clinical orientation.[30] Moreover, Lehman et al. examined these variables in the context of organizational readiness to change as opposed to counselor readiness to change.

At least three situations could have occurred to explain our results regarding clinical orientation and readiness to change counseling techniques. First, perhaps participants responded in a socially desirable manner, in that they wanted to appear ready to change. This response bias may have been elicited from informing the participants of their involvement in a study regarding the adoption of an evidence-based practice. Second, perhaps the readiness to change items were not sophisticated enough to capture readiness to change variance in our participants. This may be due to having only six items on the scale and/or the content of the items; the questions about readiness to change counseling techniques may have been too general to differentiate various levels and aspects of readiness to change. Third, as with discriminating multiform counselors, that fact that our independent variables only accounted for 8% of the variance in readiness to change scores suggests we were missing critical explanatory variables. Future researchers may want to consider (a) further validation of our readiness to change items, (b) adding items like those developed by Lehman et al.[30] to measure growth and adaptability aspects of readiness to change, and (c) examining other potentially critical variables. These additions may also help to explicate our findings that gender and race were significantly associated with readiness to change counseling techniques.

Study Limitations

Our interpretations must be considered with caution because of the limitations of our study. Most notably, our results have limited generalizability. First, we did not recruit from an exhaustive sampling frame and everybody we tried to recruit did not participate. Thus, even though a response rate of 78% was obtained, our sample may not be entirely representative of the population. However, this response rate is quite strong as compared to other mail surveys examining counselors' clinical orientations.[13,16,17] Moreover, the demographic characteristics of our respondents are similar to those found in other studies.[31,32] Another limitation pertains to our reducing the number of items on our measures to increase response rate. With this action we may have inadvertently removed important items for the research questions we examined.

Implications for Education, Supervision, and Research

Our results suggest several implications for future counselor education, supervision, and research. Assuming the clinical orientation continuum described earlier is a valid mechanism for describing clinical orientations, the continuum may serve as a useful heuristic for educators, supervisors, and researchers. Across clinical orientation studies, including the current study, clinical orientations can seemingly be classified along this traditional to contemporary continuum. Educators and supervisors may want to monitor counselors' clinical orientation development and the connection of this development to their adoption of evidence-based practices. Moreover, as educators and supervisors facilitate counselors' clinical orientation development, researchers may want to collaborate with them to further examine the relationship of clinical orientation and readiness to change, incorporating readiness to change measurement modifications noted above.

If evidence-based practices continue to evolve with changing evidence, then future efforts to further understand how counselors make constant changes seems important. We concur with the suggestion of Willenbring et al. for "quality improvement" studies of under-implemented evidence-based practices.[9] For example, examining counselors' readiness to change may accompany a quality improvement study where an evidence-based practice is merged with the predominant clinical orientations of an agency's staff.[12] Quality improvement studies like this would support the field's increasing value on being cost-effective and outcome driven as well as the value of collaboration between researchers and clinicians.[1,4]

Summary and Conclusions

Our results support the conclusion by previous researchers that counselors' clinical orientations may be becoming more complex and "challenge the description, or perhaps stereotype, of [counselors] as a monolithic group strident in its advocacy for the [traditional] disease model and closed to other treatment options."[13] Education level seems to be the most consistent discriminator of clinical orientation. Across all clinical orientation studies, counselors more contemporary in their clinical orientation tended to possess higher education levels. If contemporary orientations do indeed incorporate and reflect evidence-based practices, then our results and the results found by others support strengthening graduate level training for counselors.[13,28]

If evidence-based technology adopters are more likely to possess higher levels of education, then a relationship is suggested between clinical orientation and readiness to change.[29] Yet, we still need to learn more about how individuals' clinical orientations evolve and how readiness to change chronicles and predicts such change. If counselors' clinical orientations are indeed developmental, then readiness to change models would seem appropriate for differentiating the stages of this development. Future researchers may want to ask: Does higher education facilitate readiness to change counseling techniques and clinical orientation evolution? Or what individual characteristics predict readiness to change counseling techniques and clinical orientation evolution?

AUTHORS NOTE

The authors would like to thank Dennis McCarty, Eldon Edmundson, Mary Craighead, Katherine Bevans, and Stephen Leierer for their support on this work.

This work was funded by the Center for Substance Abuse Treatment (Grant No. TI-12906).

REFERENCES

1. Clark HW. Bridging the gap between substance abuse practice and research: The national treatment plan initiative. J Drug Iss. 2002; 32:757-68.

2. SAMHSA. SAMHSA Model programs. Downloaded from *http://modelprograms. samhsa.gov* on February 7, 2005.

3. Miller WR, Rollnick S. Motivational interviewing: Preparing people for change. New York: Guilford Press, 2002.

4. Morgenstern J, Morgan TJ, McCrady BS, et al. Manual-guided cognitive-behavioral therapy training: A promising method for disseminating empirically supported substance abuse treatments to the practice community. Psy Add Beh. 2001; 15:83-8.

5. Roman PM, Johnson JA. Adoption and implementation of new technologies in substance abuse treatment. JSAT. 2002; 22:211-18.

6. Institute of Medicine. Bridging the gap between research and practice: Forging partnerships with community-based drug and alcohol treatment. Washington, DC: National Academy Press, 1998.

7. McGlynn E, Asch S, Adams J, et al. The quality of health care delivered to adults in the United States. N Engl J Med. 2003; 348:2635-45.

8. Osborn C J, Thombs DL. Clinical orientation and sociodemographic characteristics of chemical dependency practitioners in Ohio. J Teaching Addictions. 2002; 1:5-18.

9. Willenbring ML, Kivlahan D, Kenny M, et al. Beliefs about evidence-based practices in addiction treatment: A survey of veterans administration program leaders. JSAT. 2004; 26:79-85.

10. Ball S, Bachrach K, DeCarlo J, et al. Characteristics, beliefs, and practices of community clinicians trained to provide manual-guided therapy for substance abusers. JSAT. 2002; 23:309-18.

11. Kendall P. Directing misperceptions: Researching the issues facing manual-based treatments. Clin Psy: Sci Prac. 1998; 5: 396-9.

12. McGovern MP, Fox TS, Xie H, et al. A survey of clinical practices and readiness to adopt evidence-based practices: Dissemination research in an addiction treatment system. JSAT. 2004; 26:305-12.

13. Thombs DL, Osborn CJ. A cluster analytic study of clinical orientations among chemical dependency counselors. J Coun Dev. 2001; 79:450-8.

14. Humphreys K, Greenbaum MA, Noke JM, Finney, JW. Reliability, validity, and normative data for a short version of the understanding of alcoholism scale. Psy Add Beh. 1996; 10:38-44.

15. Humphreys K, Noke JM, Moos RH. Recovering substance abuse staff members' beliefs about addiction. JSAT. 1996; 13: 75-8.

16. Morgenstern J, McCrady BS. Curative factors in alcohol and drug treatment: Behavioral and disease model perspectives. Brit J Add. 1992; 87:901-12.

17. Moyers TB, Miller WR. Therapists' conceptualizations of alcoholism: Measurement and implications for treatment decisions. Psy Add Beh. 1993; 7:238-45.

18. Toriello PJ, Hewes RL, Koch DS. Controlled drinking: Increasing counselor competency using an ethical framework. ATQ. 1997; 15:33-46.

19. Yalisove D. The origins and evolution of the disease concept of treatment. J Stud Alc. 1998; 59: 469-76.

20. Prochaska JO, DiClemente CC. The transtheoretical approach: Crossing traditional boundaries of therapy. Malabar, FL: Krieger, 1984.

21. Blondell RD, Looney SW, Hottman LM, Boaz PW. Characteristics of intoxicated trauma patients. J Add Dis. 2002; 21:1-12.

22. Littell JH, Girvin H. Stages of change: A critique. Beh Mod. 2002; 26:223-73.

23. DiClemente CC, Velasquez MM. Motivational interviewing and the stages of change. In Miller WR, Rollnick S, eds. Motivational interviewing: Preparing people for change. New York, NY: Guilford Press, 2002:201-16.

24. Miller WR, Moyers TB. The understanding of alcoholism scale. Center on Alcoholism, Substance Abuse, and Addictions, Univ of NM, Albuquerque, 1995.

25. Ogborne AC, Wild TC, Braun K, Newton-Taylor B. Measuring treatment process beliefs among staff of specialized addiction treatment services. JSAT. 1998; 15:301-12.

26. Miller WR, Tonigan JS. Assessing drinkers' motivation for change: The stages of change readiness and treatment eagerness scale (SOCRATES). Psy Add Beh. 1996; 10:81-9.

27. Hair JF, Anderson RE, Tatham RL, Black WC. Multivariate data analysis (5th ed.). Upper Saddle River, NJ: Prentice Hall, 1998.

28. Stein DM, Lambert MJ. Graduate training in psychotherapy: Are therapy outcomes enhanced? J Coun Clinical Psy. 1995; 63:182-96.

29. Rogers EM. Diffusion of innovations (4th ed.). New York, NY: The Free Press, 1995.

30. Lehman WEK, Greener JM, Simpson DD. Assessing organizational readiness for change. JSAT. 2002; 22:197-209.

31. Culbreth JR. Clinical supervision of substance abuse counselors: Current and preferred practices. J Add Offender Coun. 1999; 20:15-25.

32. Toriello PJ, Benshoff JJ. Substance abuse counselors and ethical dilemmas: The influence of recovery and education level. J Add Offender Coun. 2003; 23:83-98.

Barriers to Implementation of an Evidence-Based Practice: The Example of Methadone Maintenance

Jodie A. Trafton, PhD
Keith Humphreys, PhD
Daniel Kivlahan, PhD
Mark Willenbring, MD

SUMMARY. Research evidence supports and practice guidelines recommend methadone maintenance treatment (MMT) for opioid dependence, yet it remains controversial and is provided to a minority of

Jodie A. Trafton and Keith Humphreys are affiliated with the Center for Health Care Evaluation, Veterans Health Administration and Stanford University Medical Centers, Menlo Park, CA 94025 USA.

Daniel Kivlahan is affiliated with the Center of Excellence in Substance Abuse Treatment and Education, Veterans Health Administration Puget Sound Health Care System, Seattle, WA 98108 USA.

Mark Willenbring is affiliated with the Veterans Health Administration Medical Center, Minneapolis, MN 55417 USA.

Address correspondence to: Jodie A. Trafton, PhD, Center for Health Care Evaluation, 795 Willow Road (152-MPD), Menlo Park, CA 94025 (E-mail: Jodie.Trafton@med.va.gov).

Tha authors thank Hildi Hagedorn, Marie Kenny, and Andrea Postier for their contributions to the survey and database used in this study.

This study was supported by HSR&D and QUERI grant SUS 99-026-2, and a VA HSR&D Merit Review Entry Program award to Dr. Trafton.

[Haworth co-indexing entry note]: "Barriers to Implementation of an Evidence-Based Practice: The Example of Methadone Maintenance." Trafton, Jodie A. et al. Co-published simultaneously in *Journal of Addictive Diseases* (The Haworth Medical Press, an imprint of The Haworth Press, Inc.) Vol. 24, Supplement No. 1, 2005, pp. 93-108; and: *Implementing Evidence-Based Practices for Treatment of Alcohol and Drug Disorders* (ed: Eldon Edmundson, Jr., and Dennis McCarty) The Haworth Medical Press, an imprint of The Haworth Press, Inc., 2005, pp. 93-108. Single or multiple copies of this article are available for a fee from The Haworth Document Delivery Service [1-800-HAWORTH, 9:00 a.m. - 5:00 p.m. (EST). E-mail address: docdelivery@haworthpress.com].

Available online at http://www.haworthpress.com/web/JAD
doi:10.1300/J069v24S01_06

heroin-dependent patients. We report results of a survey about evidence-based practice guidelines of directors of addiction treatment programs in the Veterans Health Administration (VA). Compared to respondents at programs that did not provide MMT, directors of programs with MMT were more likely to be at academically affiliated medical centers, and reported greater staffing, more research experience and more confidence in clinical research. They more accurately rated the level of empirical support for 13 clinical practices for which there is varying research evidence and reported greater implementation of the most evidence-based recommendations. MMT availability was not associated with directors' attitudes toward clinical practice guidelines. We suggest that experience with and belief in clinical research is important for encouraging implementation of MMT, a controversial but empirically based treatment recommendation. *[Article copies available for a fee from The Haworth Document Delivery Service: 1-800-HAWORTH. E-mail address: <docdelivery@haworthpress. com> Website: <http://www.HaworthPress.com>]*

KEYWORDS. Opioid substitution, practice guidelines, heroin dependence, evidence-based medicine, substance abuse treatment

INTRODUCTION

Utilizing evidence-based practices has been promoted as a goal of both general and addiction medicine and significant effort has been spent to disseminate practice recommendations based upon the best of research to date. In some cases, evidence-based practices are readily incorporated into everyday clinical practice, however, this is not invariably the case. Some highly recommended evidence-based practices are rarely utilized or even offered. Methadone maintenance treatment (MMT) for heroin dependence is one such example.

Clinical practice guidelines and randomized clinical trial results seem not to have moved many treatment agencies to provide methadone maintenance.[1] As a result, only about 20% of opioid dependent individuals in the U.S. receive what research has found to be the most cost-effective and life-saving treatment,[2] and among those admitted in 2000 for treatment of heroin dependence, MMT was planned for fewer than half.[3] Even when treatment agencies provide MMT, they often do so in ways inconsistent with what science and practice guidelines recommend, for example, by not providing doses in the recommended range.[4,5] When provided in the proper manner, MMT has been shown to reduce drug use, criminal behavior, and infectious disease transmission;[6,7] however, many treatment providers remain skeptical, insisting, for example, that "you can't treat drug addiction with drugs." A recent national survey of leaders at 222 US addiction treatment programs found that MMT was rated "completely" or "somewhat" acceptable by fewer than half of respondents and only 9% reported availability of MMT at their program.[8] Thus, MMT provides an example of a treatment that, despite being well-supported by research results and highly recommended by expert consensus, has not been fully accepted into and utilized in clinical practice. To better understand how this evidence-based practice may become integrated into medical practice, we explored factors that distinguish professionals who lead programs that do provide MMT from those who do not.

Two factors seem likely to explain why some professionals provide MMT and some do not. The first is organizational. The National Institute on Drug Abuse described methadone maintenance treatment programs as "the most highly regulated form of medicine practiced in the US, as they are subject to Federal, State and local regulation."[9] Such regulations and the paperwork burden they create may vary from place to place, influencing willingness to provide methadone. Other potential barriers that may differ between agencies that have versus do not have MMT include pharmacy staffing and restrictions, local attitudes of staff in other programs, the philosophy of the agency, and available training support.

The attitudes and experience of the program director may also be influential factors. MMT directors may have different training and experience than directors of non-methadone programs, which may influence their perceptions of the value of MMT. Attitudes toward clinical research or evidence-based practice may also influence whether and how MMT is provided. In the Rosenberg survey, the most frequently cited reasons for unavailability of MMT were inconsistency with agency philosophy (44%), "a nearby agency offers it" (38%), and insufficient staff resources (30%). The "case" for MMT is both an economic and a scientific one; rigorous research supports its effectiveness for reducing substance use over at least one year and cost-effectiveness for improving life expectancy.[10-14] Relative to non-MMT directors, MMT directors may be more willing to modify clinical practices based on scientific results, either because they have greater belief in the research findings themselves or because they more strongly believe that research findings should guide practice.

As part of a VA Quality Enhancement Research initiative project focusing on translating substance use disorder (SUD) research into clinical practice, we surveyed the program director at each SUD treatment clinic within the national VA health care system regarding their beliefs and practices related to evidence-based guidelines.[15] Here we test differences in survey responses between program directors from facilities where MMT was or was not available in hopes of identifying barriers to and facilitators of providing guideline-concordant MMT within VA SUD treatment clinics. Understanding why some clinicians choose to implement MMT, an evidence-based recommendation, while others do not, may help in efforts to promote MMT and other evidence-based medicine.

MATERIALS AND METHODS

Data Collection

Each VA facility was contacted via telephone and asked to identify SUD treatment programs and their leaders. A total of 220 distinct programs were determined as being providers of autonomous services to a defined group of veterans. A pre-notice letter was mailed during October, 1999, and the 195-item surveys were mailed one week later in November, 1999. Two weeks later a reminder letter was sent, followed by a replacement survey a week later. In addition, all non-responders were contacted by telephone after the first month and new questionnaires were sent if requested. The overall response rate was 79% (174/220) at the program level and 83% at the medical center level (135/162). One survey was completed at 108 medical centers, while 27 centers had multiple program leaders responding. The centers at which multiple program leaders responded to the survey represent medical centers at which multiple substance abuse treatment programs are offered (e.g., a residential treatment program and an outpatient treatment program). In some cases, programs may collaborate to provide treatment services for their patients; for example, a residential treatment program may collaborate with an outpatient methadone maintenance clinic to provide opioid substitution treatment to their patients. Thus, in some cases, a director of a program may offer opioid substitution treatment without directing a licensed methadone clinic. As we are interested in director beliefs related to the decision to offer opioid substitution treatment to patients, all directors offering opioid substitution treatment were included in these analyses. However, for comparisons of medical center level variables, only the program treating the highest percentage of patients with opioid substitution treatment at a given medical center was considered.

The survey gathered information on the program leaders' background (gender, age, education, tenure, affiliation with a medical school, and research experience), their familiarity with specific SUD treatment guidelines, and their attitudes and opinions regarding guidelines and evidence-based practices. Included also were questions about perceived barriers to implementation of the guidelines. Respondents were asked to rate the strength of evidence for 13 specific treatment recommendations, whether or not these practices should be routinely recommended, and the current level of implementation in their program. Respondents were also asked to rate the degree to which seven specific barriers prevented them from implementing these practices in their program. Program leaders were asked to estimate the approximate percentage of unique patients who received specific treatment services, and to describe the number of full-time equivalent employees (FTEE) in their programs.

Data Analysis

Responses from directors that reported providing methadone maintenance services were compared to responses from directors that reported not offering methadone maintenance treatment within their program. ANOVA was used to compare continuous variables and Chi-square was used for categorical variables.

Strength of Evidence Ratings

Development of an Evidence Chart

Thirteen specific treatment recommendations with differing levels of empirical support were described in the survey and directors were asked to estimate the strength of evidence supporting the recommendation, their belief as to whether the recommendation should be routinely followed, and the current level of implementation of the recommendation in their program. To allow for comparison of directors responses to the actual level of empirical support for the recommendation, we developed an evidence chart describing the available research support for the recommendation. Using the chart, each of the 13 specific treatment recommendations were rated based on the strength of empirical evidence supporting the recommendation using the following scale:

Low: Minimal or negative evidence for efficacy

Medium: Positive evidence for efficacy from small trials or mixed evidence for efficacy

High: Positive evidence for efficacy from large randomized controlled trials or meta-analysis.

The evidence chart ratings were based on the following, in order of weight (Table 1):

1. Ratings from the VHA/DOD Clinical Practice Guideline for the Management of Substance Use Disorders[16]
2. Ratings from other practice guidelines
3. Results of Cochrane Reviews or other meta-analysis
4. Results from individual randomized controlled trials
5. Results from non-randomized trials

Ratings were designed to reflect evidence-based consensus of experts in addiction medicine. Recommendations that were given 1-A ratings by the VHA/DOD SUD guideline were rated High. In the cases in which the VHA/DOD guideline did not directly address the recommendation in question, recommendation of related treatments was considered. For treatments not addressed in the VHA/DOD SUD guideline, ratings by other practice guidelines and then from meta-analysis were considered. Recommendations were rated High if they were strongly recommended in practice guidelines or were found consistently effective in meta-analyses. Recommendations were rated Medium if they were given moderate or restricted recommendation in practice guidelines or were found to have mixed evidence of efficacy in meta-analyses. Recommendations were rated Low if practice guidelines recommended against use, meta-analysis found little to no evidence to support the recommendation, or there was little to no research evidence to support the efficacy of the recommendation. In cases where there was any question about the catagorization of the recommendation based upon the above criteria, the recommendation was given both ratings. In this case, survey answers that matched either rating were considered a match. This method was used to provide a more conservative comparison in cases

TABLE 1. Evidence Chart for Treatment Recommendations

Recommendation	Evidence Source	Finding	Rating
Naltrexone	1.VHA/DOD guidelines[16] 2. Meta-analysis[21] 3. Guidelines[22]	1. 1-A rating–evidence from at least one properly randomized controlled trial providing good evidence to support the recommendation be specifically considered 2. Grade A–strong and consistant evidence of efficacy in studies of large size and/or high quality 3. II–recommended w/moderate confidence	HIGH
Contingency management	1. VHA/DOD guidelines[16]	1. 1-A rating	HIGH
Verbal confrontation	1. VHA/DOD guidelines[16]	1. 1-A rating AGAINST use	LOW
Extended continuing care	1. No randomized trials/not in guideline 2. Study[23] 3. Study[24]	2. Correlation between continued use of services and better outcome 3. Active follow-up measures did not improve outcome but treatment completion did	LOW to MEDIUM
Integrated dual Dx Tx	1. Meta-analysis[25] 2. Review[26] 3. Review[27]	1. No clear evidence for advantage over usual care 2. Effective for SUD outcomes only in outpt but not inpt Tx 3. Improves Tx retention	LOW to MEDIUM
Behavioral marital therapy	1. VHA/DOD guidelines[16]	1. 1-A Rating	HIGH
Residential Tx	1. Review[28] 2. Review[29]	1. No study to date has produced evidence that residential tx is more effective than outpatient tx. 2. Neither inpatient or outpatient tx is superior	LOW
Manualized addiction Tx	1. VHA/DOD guidelines[16] 2. No effectiveness trials	1. 1-A Rating for therapies that have been manualized–no mention of use of manuals themselves.	HIGH to MEDIUM
Patient education	1. Not in guideline/No randomized trials	1. Shown to be not effective for promoting behavior change related to most chronic diseases	LOW
Smoking cessation Tx	1. Meta-analysis[30]	1. Effective with all types of nicotine replacement therapy and Bupropion	HIGH
Methadone dosing	1. VHA/DOD guidelines[16]	1. 1-A Rating	HIGH
CBT relapse prevention	1. Meta-analysis[30]	1. Generally effective with a small effect size	MEDIUM to HIGH
Disulfiram for ETOH dependence	1. VHA/DOD guideline[16] 2. Meta-analysis[31] 3. Guidelines[22]	1. Should be used selectively 2. Grade B–mixed evidence of efficacy 3. II rating for reliable motivated pts.– recommended against w/strong evidence for pts w/impulsive behavior, psychotic sx or suicidal thoughts	LOW to MEDIUM

where a strong research consensus on a recommendation does not exist. The basis for each rating is identified in the Evidence Chart (Table 1).

Comparisons of Evidence Chart Ratings to Directors' Survey Responses

Survey respondents' rating of the strength of evidence in support of each of the 13 recommendations were coded as "aware" if they matched the ratings determined in the evidence chart.

Survey respondents' rating of whether each of the 13 clinical practices should be routinely recommended were coded as "agreed" if they matched the ratings determined in the evidence chart. Survey respondents' rating of whether the 13 clinical practices were implemented in their programs were coded as "adopted" if they matched the ratings determined in the evidence chart. The number of "aware," "agreed," and "adopted" responses was determined for each survey.

Finally, respondents' estimates of the strength of evidence for each recommendation were compared to their estimation of (1) whether recommendations should be routinely recommended and (2) the clinics current level of implementation of that recommendation. Again, the total number of matching responses was determined for each survey and compared between directors offering MMT versus those who do not.

Analysis of Directors' Attitudes Towards Research and Practice Guidelines

Directors' responses to survey questions about their beliefs about randomized controlled trials and practice guidelines were analyzed and compared. Survey data were consolidated into 3 scales by taking the sum of the answers to each question in the scale (Table 2). Scales were constructed rationally, based on the predicted contribution of each survey item to the concepts measured, and were evaluated using Cronbach's alpha. A 5-point Likert scale from "Strongly disagree" to "Strongly agree" was used for questions about randomized clinical trials (RCT doubt scale) and practice guidelines (PG belief scale). A 3-point scale where 1 = not at all familiar, 2 = somewhat familiar and 3 = very familiar was used for questions in the PG familiarity scale. The questions included in each scale are as follows. The alpha statistic was calculated for each scale based on the current sample. Alphas for the scales were nearly optimized in their original conception and thus were maintained as such. Removing question 7 from the PG belief scale, would increase

TABLE 2. Scales from Survey

RCT doubt scale alpha = .71	1. In my program, clinical experience is more valid than randomized clinical trials for making treatment decisions about individual patients. 2. Program philosophy is more important than results from randomized clinical trials when deciding whether or not to implement a new technique. 3. Results of randomized clinical trials are not very useful in my program. 4. Participants in my program included in most randomized trials are too different from the patients seen in my program. 5. Providers on my staff have a professional responsibility to implement techniques shown to be effective by randomized clinical trials (REVERSE CODED).
PG belief scale alpha = .85	Evidence based practice guidelines . . . 1. promote oversimplified "cookbook" care 2. too general to apply to individual patients. 3. reduce clinicians' autonomy. 4. are too rigid to apply to individual patients. 5. do not consider clinicians' experience and judgment. 6. are useful to improve quality of care (REVERSE CODED). 7. are useful to control the cost of care (REVERSE CODED). 8. will improve outcomes if properly implemented (REVERSE CODED).
PG familiar scale alpha = 0.69	How familiar are you with the . . . 1. VA Guidelines for the Treatment of Major Depressive Disorder (MDD)? 2. VA DRAFT Guidelines for the Management of Persons with Substance Use Disorders? 3. American Psychiatric Association Clinical Practice Guidelines for the Treatment of Patients with Substance Use Disorders? 4. American Society of Addiction Medicine Patient Placement Criteria? 5. Agency for Health Care Policy & Research Clinical Practice Guidelines for Smoking Cessation? 6. Clinical Guidelines for the Management of Persons with Psychoses?

the alpha value to .86, and removing question 4 from the PG familiar scale would increase the alpha value to .695.

RESULTS

One hundred thirty-one of 174 (75%) SUD treatment directors surveyed reported that they did not offer MMT to patients at their facility. Of SUD treatment directors that offered MMT, 63% estimated that only 1-25% of patients in their clinic received MMT; only 14% estimated that 76-100% of patients received MMT. All facilities with programs offering MMT were affiliated with a medical school ($p < .001$ for difference from clinics without MMT) and a greater percentage of program directors at clinics offering MMT had been a principal investigator on a VA or NIH grant ($p = 0.009$). Clinics offering MMT had on average nearly twice as many full-time staff equivalents as did clinics not offering MMT ($p = 0.001$), with 20.6 ± 14.3 (SD) versus 10.8 ± 7.4 (SD) staff. In terms of staff composition, clinics with MMT had a greater percentage of staff employed as researchers (2.9 vs. 0.9%, p = 0.040), non-psychiatrist medical doctors (2.4 vs. 0.6%, p = 0.001), pharmacists (1.7 vs. 0.3%, p = 0.001) and RN level nurses (17.1 vs. 11.3, p = 0.017). There was a trend toward a greater percentage of staff being employed as addiction therapists (25.3 vs. 32.1%, p = 0.066) at clinics not offering MMT. There was no difference in age, years working at program, highest degree earned or the year that their highest degree was earned between directors of clinics with and without methadone maintenance programs.

Directors of SUD treatment programs that did not offer MMT reported significantly more barriers to following MMT dosing guidelines than did directors at programs that offered MMT. The total number of perceived barriers was negatively correlated with the estimated percentage of patients at the clinic who were treated with MMT (p < 0.001 for all barriers). Among directors at programs that did not offer MMT, the most commonly reported barrier to implementing MMT dosing guidelines was pharmacy/formulary restrictions (81.3%), followed by administrative barriers (75.4%), low demand or priority (70.3%), insufficient skills/knowledge (63.6%), lack of program staff time (58.5%), conflict with program philosophy (50%) and lack of confidence in effectiveness (44.9%). In clinics that did offer MMT, the most commonly reported barrier to implementing methadone dosing guidelines was conflict with program philosophy (14.3%), followed by administrative barriers (9.5%), lack of program staff time (9.5%), pharmacy/formulary restrictions (7.5%), low demand or priority (7.1%), lack of confidence in effectiveness (7.1%) and insufficient skills/knowledge (4.8%).

Directors of clinics with MMT reported greater confidence in randomized controlled trials than did directors of clinics without MMT, with directors with MMT scoring significantly lower on the RCT doubt scale (p = 0.014; MMT directors: 11.8 ± 2.9 (SD), Others: 13.2 ± 3.5). However, there was no difference between directors of clinics with and without MMT in their familiarity with or beliefs about practice guidelines, with both groups scoring similarly on the PG belief scale and the PG familiar scale.

Compared to directors of programs not offering MMT, directors of programs offering MMT were more aware of the strength of evidence supporting each clinical practice consistent with the evidence chart [p = 0.001; Number matched out of 13: MMT directors: 7.1 ± 2.3 (SD), Others: 5.9 ± 2.0 (SD)].

Similarly, directors of MMT programs agreed more consistently with the evidence chart about whether the practices should be routinely recommended [p = 0.001; Number matched out of 13: MMT directors: 6.6 ± 1.5 (SD), Others: 5.7 ± 1.5 (SD)]. Additionally, in clinics offering MMT the level of adoption in the program was more in line with the evidence chart [p = 0.049; Number matched out of 13: MMT directors: 4.9 ± 1.3 (SD), Others: 4.4 ± 1.2 (SD)].

To determine which of the recommendations directors offering MMT programs rated differently than directors not offering MMT, responses to the strength of evidence question for each recommendation was compared between these two groups of respondents. Directors with MMT programs described the strength of evidence supporting MMT dosing guidelines (p = 0.001) and manualized addiction therapy (p = 0.04) as greater than directors of programs without MMT. Directors with MMT programs also described the strength of evidence supporting patient education as an intervention as lower than did directors of programs without MMT (p = 0.04).

For both MMT and non-MMT directors, their judgments on whether the recommendations should be routinely recommended were strongly/ significantly associated with their estimation of the strength of evidence (r = .662, p < .001 and r = .529, p < .001 for MMT and non-MMT, respectively). However, directors' report of implementing recommendations in their clinics was not as strongly correlated with their estimation of the strength of evidence (r = .036, p > .05 and r = .191, p < .05 for MMT and non-MMT, respectively); these variables were not correlated in MMT directors' report.

DISCUSSION

Directors of clinics offering MMT reported relatively few barriers to provision of guideline concordant MMT treatment at their facility. Directors not offering MMT, however, reported numerous barriers to providing guideline concordant methadone maintenance treatment, with six of seven listed barriers being rated by greater than 50% of the directors as a significant barrier to following recommended methadone dosing guidelines. This might be explained by the significant start-up work that would be required to begin offering MMT in a SUD program such as obtaining regulatory approvals, re-organizing clinic structure and staff re-training. Methadone maintenance treatment programs are subject to additional regulatory requirements and require additional staff knowledge of and training in methadone prescribing and dosing techniques; the effort involved in acquiring these additional trainings and approvals may be prohibitive. Recent changes in the regulations and regulatory bodies overseeing provision of MMT that occurred after administration of this survey, attempt to reduce this burden somewhat.[17] It would be interesting to see whether these regulatory changes reduced directors' perceptions of barriers to provision of MMT. Alternatively, lack of experience using methadone maintenance for treatment of substance use disorders may result in exaggerated perceptions of impediments to its use. In this case, exposing directors to methadone maintenance treatment, by means of a short, training visit to a substance use disorders clinic that does offer MMT for example, might significantly reduce the perceived barriers to implementing MMT as recommended by the guidelines. Further investigation could distinguish the contribution of these two possibilities to the low level of MMT implementation in VA substance use disorders programs and could guide intervention techniques to increase MMT implementation in clinics currently not offering this treatment option.

Programs offering MMT tended to be larger, with twice the number of staff as programs without MMT. They were more research affiliated, employing a greater percentage of research staff, being more likely to have a director with experience as principal investigator on a VA or NIH grant, and universally being affiliated with a medical school. Greater exposure to and participation in research appears to favor implementation of methadone maintenance treatment in substance use disorder treatment programs. One would suspect that university-affiliated programs have greater access to new scientific findings, and perhaps more support for implementing those findings into practice.

Directors offering MMT versus not, also differed in their belief in and knowledge of clinical research. Directors not offering MMT expressed less confidence in the validity of, usefulness of and need to implement findings from randomized clinical trials. Interestingly, however, they do not differ in their beliefs about or familiarity with clinical practice guidelines. It would thus appear that these clinic directors do not generally mistrust practice recommendations, but rather selectively doubt findings from controlled clinical research studies. It would be interesting to know whether directors have different opinions about guidelines based on research evidence versus clinician consensus depending on their research training and experience.

It is not possible from this study to distinguish whether clinicians' doubts about research results stem from a lack of understanding and inability to access research results or an informed criticism of the research process based upon its limitations. It is possible that non-MMT directors are aware of research findings, but view the quality and objectiveness of MMT and possibly other addiction research as low. These two possibilities would constitute different problems for increasing provision of MMT and other evidence-based medicine. The fact that the directors not offering MMT did not consistently rate the strength of evidence for recommendations as lower than the evidence-ratings from the evidence chart would favor the interpretation that their unease with research findings was due more to lack of awareness of research than to a systematic criticism of the quality of clinical research. Conversely, 44.9% of non-MMT directors reported that lack of confidence in the effectiveness of MMT, which could indicate that these clinicians consider the research to be of poor quality. In any case, we cannot definitively distinguish between these possibilities from our survey results.

Additionally, as this is a cross-sectional study, we cannot determine whether increased research knowledge or participation is causally related to the choice to offer MMT, a third variable may be responsible for the association. It is possible that, for example, MMT is more likely to be offered in major urban areas where both heroin use and medical research activities are concentrated. Randomized trials of interventions to increase research participation or understanding are necessary to determine if this association is causal.

Nevertheless, the hypothesis that lack of belief and participation in research is associated with having less accurate knowledge of the evidence base for practice recommendations and less implementation of evidence-based practices is consistent with findings of studies investigating barriers to implementation of evidence-based practices amongst nurses. Difficulty interpreting research findings and lack of time and ability to effectively read and apply research results have been identified as significant barriers to implementation of evidence-based practices.[18,19] Substance use disorder clinic directors may be hindered by similar difficulties. Notably, a trial that randomized staff nurses to high, low or control participation in clinical research groups found that nurses that participated in research (at either the high or low level) showed more implementation of research in practice than controls, as measured by the Research Utilization Questionnaire.[20] Taken together, this suggests that the association between increased research participation and increased use of evidence-based practices, may be more than simple correlation, and that active efforts to include clinicians in clinical research (as is underway in the National Institute on Drug Abuse Clinical Trials Network, for example) will encourage the translation of research results into practice.

The personal beliefs of clinicians will inevitably influence their treatment decisions. MMT has historically been a controversial treatment, and has evoked significant ethical and political debate over the years. Clinicians may have developed strong personal beliefs about MMT that may or may not be consistent with the findings of clinical research. When personal beliefs and clinical research findings disagree, clinicians must choose to follow one or the other. We suggest that greater participation in or understanding of clinical research may encourage clinicians to follow the research based recommendations rather than their personal beliefs.

Thus, efforts to encourage participation in and understanding of research methodology and findings amongst management level clinicians may be particularly important for the translation of complicated or controversial evidence-based clinical practices like MMT. Familiarity with practice guidelines was not restricted to those who demonstrated more accurate knowledge of research evidence. The guidelines may be accepted and put into practice by clinicians with and without experience and strong belief in research when the recommendations agree with clinicians currently held beliefs or *"common sense"* expectations. Clinicians without research experience, however, may be less swayed by research evidence that suggests practices contrary to the clinicians' current beliefs. This might explain why the biggest differences in the estimation of the strength of the evidence base for recommendations between the more research-experienced methadone providers and the non-methadone providers occurred for the recommendations on methadone dosing and patient education. Methadone maintenance treatment is controversial despite extensive research evidence for its efficacy,[10-12] and patient education rarely evokes criticism despite copious research demonstrating its lack of effect in changing health behaviors. Without confidence in accessing, interpreting and evaluating research results, clinicians may be hesitant to accept counterintuitive or stigmatized practices (e.g., methadone maintenance) or to admit that a treatment with intuitive appeal is not helpful (e.g., patient education).

In conclusion, difficulty with regulatory requirements and lack of training are associated with low implementation of MMT. Efforts to encourage incorporation of research findings on methadone maintenance treatment into substance use disorders treatment have been more successful amongst clinicians with a solid belief in and experience with research. Novel dissemination techniques may be necessary to reach those who are less research experienced. We hypothesize that the hesitancy of less research-experienced clinicians to accept and adopt evidence based-recommendations for opioid substitution treatment may generalize to other recommendations that lack intuitive appeal.

REFERENCES

1. SAMHSA Office of Applied Studies. Drug and Alcohol Information Series: S-13 Uniform Facilities Data Set (UFDS):1999 Data on Substance Abuse Treatment Facilities. 2001; *http://wwwdasis.samhsa.gov/99ufds/ufds1999report.pdf.* website accessed on 11/19/03.

2. Fiellin DA, Rosenheck RA, Kosten TR. Office-based treatment for opioid dependence: reaching new patient populations. Am J Psychiatry. 2001; 158: 1200-1204.

3. SAMHSA Office of Applied Studies. Treatment Episode Data Set (TEDS): 1992-2001. National Admissions to Substance Abuse Treatment Services, DASIS Series: S-20, DHHS Publication No. (SMA) 03-3778, Rockville MD, 2003.

4. D'Aunno T, Folz-Murphy N, Lin X. Changes in methadone treatment practices: results from a panel study, 1988-1995. Am J Drug Alcohol Abuse. 1999; 25: 681-699.

5. D'Aunno T, Pollack HA. Changes in methadone treatment practices: results from a national panel study, 1988-2000. JAMA. 2002; 288: 850-856.

6. Trafton JA, Barnett P, Finney J, Moos R, Willenbring M, Humphreys K. Effective treatment for opioid dependence. Practice Matters. 2001; 6: 1-6.

7. Zaric GS, Barnett PG, Brandeau ML. HIV transmission and the cost-effectiveness of methadone maintenance. Am J Public Health. 2000; 90: 1100-1111.

8. Rosenberg H, Phillips KT. Acceptability and availability of harm-reduction interventions for drug abuse in American substance abuse treatment agencies. Psychology of Addictive Behaviors. 2003; 17: 203-210.

9. NIDA. Buprenorphine Update: Question and Answers. 2001; *http://165.112.78.61.* website accessed on 11/19/03.

10. Ling W, Charuvastra C, Kaim SC, Klett CJ. Methadyl acetate and methadone as maintenance treatments for heroin addicts. A veterans administration cooperative study. Arch Gen Psychiatry. 1976; 33: 709-720.

11. Newman RG, Whitehill W.B. Double-blind comparison of methadone and placebo maintenance treatments of narcotic addicts in Hong Kong. Lancet. 1979; 2: 485-488.

12. Sees KL, Delucchi KL, Masson C, Rosen A, Clark HW, Robillard H, Banys P, Hall SM. Methadone maintenance vs. 180-day psychosocially enriched detoxification for treatment of opioid dependence: a randomized controlled trial. JAMA. 2000; 283: 1303-1310.

13. Barnett PG. The cost-effectiveness of methadone maintenance as a health care intervention. Addiction. 1999; 94: 479-488.

14. Barnett PG, Hui SS. The cost-effectiveness of methadone maintenance. Mt Sinai J Med. 2000; 67: 365-374.

15. Willenbring ML, Kivlahan D, Grillo M, Kenny M, Hagedorn H, Postier A. Program leaders' attitudes and perceptions regarding evidence based practices in addiction treatment. J Substance Abuse Treatment. 2004; 26: 79-85.

16. VA/DoD Evidence-Based Clinical Practice Guideline Working Group. VA/DoD Clinical Parctice Guideline for Management of Substance Use Disorders in Primary and Specialty Care Settings, v 1.0. Washington, DC: Office of Quality and Performance, Department of Veterans Affairs, 2001. *http://www.oqp.med.va.gov/cpg/SUD/SUD_Base.htm.* accessed on 4/6/04.

17. Department of Health and Human Services SAMHSA. Opioid Drugs in Maintenance and Detoxification Treatment of Opiate Addiction; Final Rule. Federal Register. 2001; 66: 4076-4102.

18. Bryar RM, Closs SJ, Baum G, Cooke J, Griffiths J, Hostick T, Kelly S, Knight S, Marshal K, Thompson DR. Yorkshire BARRIER project. The Yorkshire BARRIERS project: diagnostic analysis of barriers to research utilization. Int J Nurs Stud. 2003; 40: 73-84.

19. Sitzia J. Barriers to research utilization: the clinical setting and nurses themselves. Intensive Crit Care Nurs. 2002; 18: 230-243.

20. Tranmer JE, Lochhaus-Gerlach J, Lam M. The effect of staff nurse participation in a clinical nursing research project on attitude towards, access to, support of and use of research in the acute care setting. Can J Nurs Leadersh. 2002; 15: 18-26.

21. Garbutt JC, West SL, Carey TS, Lohr KN, Crews FT. Pharmacological treatment of alcohol dependence: a review of the evidence. JAMA. 1999; 281: 1318-1325.

22. American Psychiatric Association. Practice Guidelines for the Treatment of Psychiatric Disorders Compendium 2002. Washington DC: American Psychiatric Association, 2002.

23. Moos R, Schaefer J, Andrassy J, Moos B. Outpatient mental health care, self-help groups, and patients' one-year treatment outcomes. J Clin Psychol. 2001; 57: 273-287.

24. Gilbert FS. The effect of type of aftercare follow-up on treatment outcome among alcoholics. J Stud Alcohol. 1988; 49: 149-159.

25. Ley A, Jeffery DP, McLaren S, Siegfried N. Treatment programmes for people with both severe mental illness and substance misuse. Cochrane Database Syst Rev. 2000; CD001088.

26. Drake RE, Mercer-McFadden C, Mueser KT, McHugo GJ, Bond GR. Review of integrated mental health and substance abuse treatment for patients with dual disorders. Schizophr Bull. 1998; 24: 589-608.

27. Hellerstein DJ, Rosenthal RN, Miner CR. Integrating services for schizophrenia and substance abuse. Psychiatr Q. 2001; 72: 291-306.

28. Miller WR, Hester RK. Inpatient alcoholism treatment. Who benefits? Am Psychol. 1986; 41: 794-805.

29. Cole SG, Lehman WE, Cole EA, Jones A. Inpatient vs. outpatient treatment of alcohol and drug abusers. Am J Drug Alcohol Abuse. 1981; 8: 329-345.

30. Silagy C, Lancaster T, Stead L, Mant D, Fowler G. Nicotine replacement therapy for smoking cessation. Cochrane Database Syst Rev. (4). 2002; CD000146.

31. Irvin JE, Bowers CA, Dunn ME, Wang MC. Efficacy of relapse prevention: a meta-analytic review. J Consult Clin Psychol. 1999; 67: 563-570.

Index

BOOK ORDER FORM!

Order a copy of this book with this form or online at:
http://www.HaworthPress.com/store/product.asp?sku=5762

Implementing Evidence-Based Practices for Treatment of Alcohol and Drug Disorders

____ in softbound at $16.95 ISBN-13: 978-0-7890-3152-5 / ISBN-10: 0-7890-3152-3.
____ in hardbound at $24.95 ISBN-13: 978-0-7890-3151-8 / ISBN-10: 0-7890-3151-5.

COST OF BOOKS ____

POSTAGE & HANDLING ____
US: $4.00 for first book & $1.50
for each additional book
Outside US: $5.00 for first book
& $2.00 for each additional book.

SUBTOTAL ____

In Canada: add 7% GST. ____

STATE TAX ____
CA, IL, IN, MN, NJ, NY, OH, PA & SD residents
please add appropriate local sales tax.

FINAL TOTAL ____
If paying in Canadian funds, convert
using the current exchange rate,
UNESCO coupons welcome.

❑**BILL ME LATER:**
Bill-me option is good on US/Canada/
Mexico orders only; not good to jobbers,
wholesalers, or subscription agencies.

❑**Signature** ____

❑ **Payment Enclosed: $** ____

❑ **PLEASE CHARGE TO MY CREDIT CARD:**
❑Visa ❑MasterCard ❑AmEx ❑Discover
❑Diner's Club ❑Eurocard ❑JCB

Account # ____

Exp Date ____

Signature ____
(Prices in US dollars and subject to change without notice.)

PLEASE PRINT ALL INFORMATION OR ATTACH YOUR BUSINESS CARD

Name	
Address	
City	State/Province	Zip/Postal Code
Country	
Tel	Fax
E-Mail	

May we use your e-mail address for confirmations and other types of information? ❑Yes ❑No We appreciate receiving
your e-mail address. Haworth would like to e-mail special discount offers to you, as a preferred customer.
We will never share, rent, or exchange your e-mail address. We regard such actions as an invasion of your privacy.

Order from your **local bookstore** or directly from
The Haworth Press, Inc. 10 Alice Street, Binghamton, New York 13904-1580 • USA
Call our toll-free number (1-800-429-6784) / Outside US/Canada: (607) 722-5857
Fax: 1-800-895-0582 / Outside US/Canada: (607) 771-0012
E-mail your order to us: orders@HaworthPress.com

For orders outside US and Canada, you may wish to order through your local
sales representative, distributor, or bookseller.
For information, see http://HaworthPress.com/distributors

(Discounts are available for individual orders in US and Canada only, not booksellers/distributors.)

The Haworth Press Inc.

Please photocopy this form for your personal use.
www.HaworthPress.com

BOF05